Getting Past the Past

Stepping Out of Your Emotional Prison ... Forever

Joyce Oglesby

Getting Past the Past
Stepping Out of Your Emotional Prison ... Forever

Joyce Oglesby has been married to her pastor husband, Webby, for 40 years. They have two married daughters, and five grandchildren. Joyce has been a business owner in her career as a court reporter for over 30 years.

Joyce has authored several books designed to strengthen and preserve the family unit. As a result, she served as a relationship expert on a local secular television program, is currently a Q&A columnist in a regional women's magazine, and the talk-show host of the popular radio show *Just Ask Joyce*™.

Joyce is a motivational and inspirational speaker, addressing women, men, couples, and teens across the nation connecting real life with family values.

For more information or to contact Joyce to speak to your group or organization, go to www.justaskjoyce.com.

ISBN#: 978-1466405066

Published by: CreateSpace and The Local Wordsmith

Getting Past the Past

Stepping Out of Your Emotional Prison ... Forever

Joyce Oglesby

Dedication

To Lola, my mother, …

who lived to love, loved to live, and died because both had taken their toll.

Acknowledgement

There are countless success stories throughout the ages attributable to the efforts of The Gideons. Only until the story becomes personal can one fully appreciate the significance of obedience to The Great Commission. I might have never come to know the complete and glorious pardon of Jesus Christ had that Bible not been placed in my hand by a devoted man of God in elementary school. I don't remember the gentleman's name, nor could I give you an accurate description of his features. I do, however, recall his face being kind, compassionate, and welcoming.

I was one of the more fortunate. I have often wondered the path my life would have taken had I not been introduced to my Savior through the pages of my Gideons Bible. Countless times I've opened the drawer to a motel nightstand/desk and found the Gideons Bible there. Initially, my thoughts were that I might claim the Bible to replace the one discarded by my father. I was convicted, however, that there could be some lost soul who might occupy this room in the future. What if this Bible never got replaced? I would have dimmed the torch of personal evangelism the three traveling founders of The Gideons began on July 1, 1899.

I will never be the hallmark to the world like The Gideons International. I will, however, like countless others it has touched, leave behind a watermark to its legacy.

~~~

"The sower sows the word."
~Mark 4:14 (NAS)

Table of Contents

Part 2: Fugitive in the Present

Part 3: Pardoned for the Future

Let's Do It

My producer Tom leans his head into my sound booth at the radio station and says, "Three minutes till we go live, Joyce."

I look up from scattered pencils and notepads. "I'm set. Let's do it."

Already my incoming call lines are lighting up like a Christmas tree. When I first started doing "Just Ask Joyce™" as a Sunday afternoon filler, I had only a smattering of listeners. But word spread fast, and within six weeks I was on the air five days a week from my base station in Louisville, Kentucky scrambling for guests, and each day I started to get flooded with text messages, phone calls, letters, cards, and emails.

In the fleeting seconds prior to starting my show, I take a moment to scan some of the text messages and emails that are coming in this day:

"My daughter is pregnant and only in the ninth grade, Joyce, and I don't know whether to hold her tightly or send her to a girls' home in another state. Tell me what to do."

"My wife flirts with other men. She says it's just for fun, but I'm jealous. Who's wrong here, Joyce?"

"Our church is going through a split. It's breaking my heart. Our pastor is old, and the younger people want modern music and more contemporary messages. But this pastor did the baptisms of our children and performed their wedding ceremonies. I feel I owe him my loyalty. Is there any hope for our congregation, Joyce?"

"Oh, Joyce, I've done something so terrible, I'll never be able to forgive myself. If it ever gets out, I'll be ruined. But even if it doesn't get out, I'm dying of guilt and shame. How can I make amends with God over what I've done? Please, talk about this today on your show."

So many difficulties, so little air time. And, besides, who am I to think that I can solve the problems of the world? *Me* – a hick farm girl from Georgia who married at 19, no college degree, and had to deal with her own inner demons for more than two decades before finding peace and resolution.

But maybe that's it. My listeners aren't looking for an M.D. in psychiatry or a Ph.D. in psychology (although I have fun with these good folks when they are guests on my show from time to time). What my listeners relate to is someone who has "been there, felt that." And that's me, and that's why every day they "Just Ask Joyce."

I was first raped at age five. I was worked from predawn hours until after sunset all my childhood, helping my family eke out an existence on a tobacco farm. I was mocked by my elementary teachers, shunned by the other students, and not included with the in-crowd. I had to sit alone on the bus ride home and rush through my homework, knowing there'd be no time for books and lessons once I got home. I was bullied by a drunken father, whipped by a love-starved malnourished mom who had birthed eight children, and "farmed out" to neighbors if there was ever any extra money to be earned.

My listeners know this about me. I've shared it on the air. I've shared it in the books I have written. I've shared it at the women's retreats, church rallies, and national conventions I've spoken at. To know that I found Christ and drew my strength from Him as a way of clawing my way out of that horrendous childhood serves as a beacon of light in many a person's dark world. "If Joyce did it, maybe I can, too," they tell themselves.

Tom's voice comes over the intercom. "Ten-second countdown, Joyce. I'm cueing the theme music."

I pull the microphone close to my mouth. I listen as Nichole Nordeman's *Legacy* alerts showtime. I close my eyes and begin the show as I always do, silently praying, "Lord, let this be to Your Glory. You promised me, 'Now go, and I will speak for you and teach you what to say.' Bless people today, Lord. Let my voice reflect that it's all about You!"

"Annndddd ... welcome to 'Just Ask Joyce.' I'm Joyce Oglesby, your host of this family nourishment hour. I'll be taking your calls *live* in a few minutes. But first, many of you have asked me to give you more information about my life...my childhood...my upbringing. To that request, I'm now ready to say, it's ready to share with you. Let's go back together."

> *Don't allow unwelcome consequences from poor judgment to enslave you.*

Part I

Prisoner to the Past

1

Prisoner to the Past

Fearfully and Wonderfully Made

O Lord, you have searched me, and you know me. You know when I sit and when I rise; you perceive my thoughts from afar. You discern my going out and my lying down; you are familiar with all my ways. Before a word is on my tongue, you know it completely, O Lord. You hem me in—behind and before; you have laid your hand upon me. Such knowledge is too wonderful for me, too lofty for me to attain. Where can I go from your Spirit? Where can I flee from your presence? If I go up to the heavens, you are there; if I make my bed in the depths, you are there. If I rise on the wings of the dawn, if I settle on the far side of the sea; even there your hand will guide me, your right hand will hold me fast. If I say, "Surely the darkness will hide me and the light become night around me," even the darkness will not be dark to you; the night will shine like the day, for darkness is as light to you.

For you created my inmost being; you knit me together in my mother's womb. I praise you because I am fearfully and wonderfully made; your works are wonderful, I know that full well. My frame was not hidden from you when I was made in the secret place. When I was woven together in the depths of the earth, your eyes saw my unformed body. All the days ordained for me were written in your book before one of them came to be. How precious to me are your thoughts, O God! How vast is the sum of them! Were I to count them, they would outnumber the grains of sand. When I awake, am still with you. If only you would slay the wicked, O God! Away from me, you bloodthirsty men! They speak of you with evil intent; your adversaries misuse your name. Do I not hate those who hate you, O Lord, and abhor those who rise up against you? I have nothing but hatred for them; I count them my enemies.

Search me, O God, and know my heart; test me and know my anxious thoughts. See if there is any offensive way in me, and lead me in the way everlasting.

~Psalm 139, NIV

~ ~ ~

"Lord, you knit me together in the womb? Really? All the days intended for me were written in your book? You knew I would go through this today? You knew, yet you allowed it? Why? Please, Lord God, tell me why." And the little girl wept. And she wept. And she wept....

~ ~ ~

Tears were not unusual for me as a child. Unlike they are today. Childhood. It was a different way of life. A far-away time through which I would never live. Indeed, I would miss that part of life. It would be taken from me. I would never catch up to that component of existence. Once the day escapes, none of us can ever return. Except in our minds. But, many memories of my childhood were always too painful to visit. To think about it was a reminder of who I was: a nobody who mattered to no one. Try as I might to break free from the stigma of being an insignificant person, the thought would keep me hostage for many years.

I was weak as a child. Not in stamina. Working on a farm kept me fit. Numerous, arduous hours would find this young girl performing tasks an adult man should carry out. Oh, no. My muscular strength surpassed my age and gender. I was small in stature but could handle a grizzly when necessary. My weakness was hidden from the world. Unless someone looked into my eyes to glimpse the hollow, desolate stare, no one would see the prevailing flaw underneath the surface. My thin but toned body was even more depraved within. There had been years of malnutrition for the soul. Days were too hard. Nights were even more difficult. Who would help me? I considered running away, but I couldn't leave Mother. She was the one who suffered most. And then, what about the others? It was hard for my seven siblings, too. Surely people saw the evidence. Didn't they know I couldn't ask for help? They would have to come to me. But did anyone care? If they did, no one dared show it. I was confused. Lonely. Loveless. Deplete of contentment.

Children weren't supposed to hurt, were they? *I had never known anything else.* They weren't supposed to witness Daddy beat up Mama. *I can't remember days it didn't happen.* They shouldn't have to dread the day upon waking. *Daybreak seldom brought peace.* A child shouldn't have to wait for the next altercation; shouldn't have to speculate as to whom would be its latest victim. *There was always at least one.* Children shouldn't have to fear falling asleep. Sleep should blanket them with comfort and rest. *Not wake them with violating fear.* A child is born to be carefree. Not nervous. He or she should be nurtured. *Not tortured.* Children are born to live. *Not wish they could die.*

A Real Hero

The Gideons are heroes to many. I am but one life spared. My freedom march began when they placed a Bible in my hand after elementary chapel. I often wonder how many children's lives would have been changed had one voice been silenced in 1960. By 1963, Madelyn Murray O'Hair would shut the prison cell door on countless broken victims of abuse and other daunting injustices. Incalculable wayward souls would never find the key to unlock the shackles that kept them hostage to a distasteful past. If I failed to share how God redeemed me, what a disservice it would be to the bold and tenacious calling of the Gideon organization. It is because of its love for Christ that today I can share my liberating testimony.

The Bible the Gideons placed in my hands became a source of comfort to me from that moment. A flashlight underneath my covers provided light to the source of illumination for my soul. It was through these pages of script written centuries ago by persecuted men of God that I would begin to strengthen my mind, nourish my soul, and heal my brokenness. These words protected me as a child.

It was difficult reading for a young, untrained mind. The Old Testament was challenging. Yet, its stories were revealing. Could such things have really happened? Creation? The flood? An ocean parted with a shepherd's staff? A great-grandmother (in a child's mind) giving birth in her nineties? A big fish swallowing a man and the man living to tell about it? Such intrigue was foreign to my immature knowledge.

The book of Psalms brought sweet comfort. Proverbs offered great wisdom.

The New Testament pounded on the door of my heart. Once I opened it, its message came rushing in with the greatest of force. Its power was alarming. Its message was bold. Clumsily, I scoured pages of history about a man who was hanged on a cross.

Wait a minute! Is this the same one the prophet spoke of in the book of Isaiah? He died for sinners. Was I one of those?

I was familiar with this name as a child. When we went to my Grandpa Suggs' church, he would preach about this Jesus. *We only went on special occasions.* His was a message of fire and brimstone, of eternal damnation, and he shouted to the top of his lungs about how people would be cast into the flames of hell. He frightened me, but I didn't understand why.

This Jesus was the same man my sweet Granddaddy Noles would sing about as I sat in his lap and he played his piano for me. *We hadn't been allowed back into his home for a while by now. I missed those special moments with him.*

The four-letter words in the New Testament easily rolled off the palate. They were words of simplicity. These expressions gave life a new meaning for a third-grader. Terms like hope, love, true, and pure. I understood strength, noble, right, and even excellent. Philippians quickly became my favorite section of this testament. I would read its message over and over, grasping new meaning with each reading. It was exciting to me. My banner verse would be chosen from this book. It would become my stronghold for new purpose in life.

~~~

> Finally, brothers, whatever is true, whatever is noble, whatever is right, whatever is lovely, whatever is admirable – if anything is excellent or praiseworthy – think about such things.
>
> ~Philippians 4:8 (NIV)

You Know Me

How God could know I would need the message in these words before He even breathed life into me was fascinating to my young mind. This new hope was like a fairytale. It became a dream wrapping up my mind but not yet tying the ribbon. It had not collected the part of me essential for the complete package. There would be other days and more studying of the scripture. There would be other people to intersect my path in order for my heart to understand fully how the promises scrolled on these pages so long ago would be fulfilled in my life. It was the beginning of a process. In due course I would learn how I was fearfully and wonderfully made and was made fit to become an heir in the Kingdom of God. But in the meantime, life would be difficult.

> *Once the day escapes, none of us can ever return. Except in our minds.*

2

Part 1: Prisoner to the Past

Something in a Name

> "Human history is the long terrible story of man trying to find something other than God which will make him happy."
>
> ~C.S. Lewis

I would be the only child my father would name. At least, under duress. My mother didn't mind the "Mary" part. After all, she had a heart for my father's mother. Grandma Mary was a beaten-down woman, as well, from what I've come to learn. Her preacher husband would disguise his true nature with the cloak of Christ. God's good reputation has been marred by many men like my grandfather claiming His likeness. Knowing a bit about my grandfather's heavy hand sheds light on the passed-down qualities his sons acquired. There were some good traits about my dad's father, though. He was likable and well-respected by his peers, from all indications. None of that esteem measured up to those who never received such favor of his kindness. I must say, however, Grandpa Willie never raised a hand to me. Not even a gentle one.

Grandma Mary was a good soul. Quiet in spirit. A submissive, subdued demeanor often accompanied her drooped countenance. She never had time to give special love. I don't remember her even so much as patting my head. I never recall her visiting in our home. *Then again, not many people did throughout the years. The kids were afraid to bring anyone in for fear of what they might witness.* Grandma Mary was busy scurrying about the home the infrequent times we visited. She had a bedraggled look, slumped over at a young age. A servant to all; slave to her husband. I never saw her smile. I can only imagine why. Cancer would claim her life early in my childhood. Grandma Mary was a minimal figure in my life; yet, I feel honored today to be her namesake.

~~~

When I hear the name Mary, I don't think of my grandmother first, nor do I reflect on it being my first name. My thoughts immediately turn to Mary, the mother of our Savior. I've often wondered, had I changed my given name later in life, could I have lived up to its character? Not that of Grandma Mary, but of Mary, the Mother of Jesus. Could I have mirrored her qualities? It would have been a lot to live up to.

I believe Mary, the mother of our Savior, was a woman just like me — many women rolled into one. But Mary was set apart. No one would ever achieve her calling in life. No woman will ever enjoy the position Mary has. Yeah, not even Mother Teresa. Mary would be revered above all women, for she had found high favor of the Lord.

We don't know a lot about Mary. She's sprinkled all throughout the New Testament, although not in large degrees. But she would play a significant role. The glimpses we are afforded of her provide us with depths of knowledge from the scattering of words about her character and faith. She was humble — just a girl from Nazareth with no social status. She was thoughtful — she pondered things in her heart. She was spiritual — she knew God so intimately that she recognized His greatness in all things. Mary was also submissive — she understood the great cost involved, yet relentlessly followed God's will. Mary was courageous — she acted impulsively, taking on her assignment without fear of the consequences. She was hungry for knowledge — she sought guidance and counsel from the godly. Oh, yes, Mary was faithful. She was a blessed one. She was truly highly favored by God. It would behoove us all to aspire to emulate her qualities.

~ ~ ~

Inherited Names

It was the "Joyce" part of my name my mother would struggle with. For years she only called me "Josephine." Her parents would address me as "Suzie" (with a Z for zing!). I didn't mind that name. It suited me better than Joyce. It was cute and sassy, and I loved it. But then, I loved Mother's parents, especially my granddaddy. He thawed my heart and dusted momentary twinkles in my eyes.

It would be years before I would understand the reasoning behind the multiple names I had inherited. Mother would share with me later, however, it was with much contempt she was forced to name me "Joyce." She could not bring herself to call me by my name. It was the same name as one of my father's girlfriends. Her objection was duly noted.

I was the third child born to a family of eight, only five years into their marriage. There had been many mistresses prior to my birth, and they would be too numerous to mention throughout the years. Certainly there had been more adulterous relationships than years of marriage between the two. My dad was a real son of a preacher man. He was following in his father's footsteps, and his view of a woman's worth would be skewed to this day.

I was the first girl, and it would have been grand to be a "daddy's girl." It's a given territory – an honor that comes without merit, much like moms and their sons. I feel secure in speaking for my baby sister, the youngest in the family, when I say that Kathy, likewise, would have enjoyed that position in life. Neither of us experienced the grandeur of this blessed position of our assigned gender, although I was the only one in the family who could "manage" Dad. Perhaps it was because of my protective heart for others.

~~~

Children are special gifts from God. Their heart's desire is to bond with their parents – both parents. Securing a place in a special chamber of a mommy and/or daddy's heart is essential for every child's emotional health. That is the source of nourishment that will feed a child's consciousness. It is life-sustaining. Not in the physical sense of sustenance, but certainly the emotional. God's instruction is rich with direction for parents. He speaks of grave consequences when we, as parents, neglect our role to protect His children.

~~~

At that time the disciples came to Jesus and asked, "Who is the greatest in the kingdom of heaven?" He called a little child and had him stand among them. And he said: "I tell you the truth, unless you change and become like little children, you will never enter the kingdom of heaven. Therefore, whoever humbles himself like this child is the greatest in the kingdom of heaven. And whoever welcomes a little child like this in my name welcomes me. But if anyone causes one of these little ones who believe in me to sin, it would be better for him to have a large millstone hung around his neck and to be drowned in the depths of the sea."
~Matthew 18:1-6 (NIV)

~~~

Time Brings Understanding

I didn't know the details behind Mary, Joyce, Josephine, and Suzie. It would be awhile before the particulars would surface. When it did, I began to understand the contempt in Mother's voice when she would yell for me to come. "Josephine!" The "phine" would climb three octaves as she got my attention. I came to miss the sound of it as she worked through the issue of her lack of input in the name selection process. I was her first girl, too. It would have been appropriate that she have some voice in choosing a name for each of her children, and especially her daughter.

Mother went from Josephine to Joyce, but she adopted her own unique style of saying it. "Joe-wess," she would call out. It would grate on my nerves. "It's Joyce," I would tell her, "with no 'wess.' Like Joy, and then a soft C."

After much time and maturity, I grew to love the way she pronounced my name. I would grow in patience. My heart would begin to take on the pangs of being a woman. I connected the dots of how painful it must have been that she would be deprived of a voice in any decision, ever. I began to understand how some of the things I will share with you could occur, yet my womanhood also brought more confusion as to why they did.

However, I didn't come to a full appreciation of her drawn-out version of my name until she died. Now, I'd give anything to hear her grating tone of "Joe-wess." Odd, isn't it, how many of us overlook the gift in a name. When I could hear her say it, as irritating a sound to me as it had been for such a long period of time, at least I had her to talk to. It was a gift that she called me by name. It was a gift that she had sacrificed and given me life. It was her hand that had written my name on the birth certificate. My name was chosen as a part of this family, regardless of the circumstances surrounding it.

~~~

What a great parallel to the story of redemption and grace. I have been called by name. Singled out by Jesus. He sacrificed to give me life. It is His hand that has written my name in the Lamb's Book of Life. It doesn't matter what baggage accompanies my re-birth; my name has been announced as a part of the Family of God.

~~~

A New Name

So it was with the story behind my name. But, I would begin to learn a very significant name in the course of my history. This name of Jesus, to whom the Gideons had introduced me, would come to bring me worth. His name would soon hold great meaning in my life. His name would soon set grace around mine. I would come to appreciate that possessing a number of names would mean more than confusion. Jesus, Savior, Lord, Messiah, Redeemer, Friend. Like myself, He was called by various titles. The greatness attached to His names would bear significance to me. I was too young to know all He was and everything He could do for me and through me. *I may never grow into the richness of this knowledge. It is a continual learning process.* I would not even understand why He would love me so much that He gave His life for me. But, I would not rest until I knew more about this Jesus. There *is* something in a name.

~~~

But the angel said to her, "Do not be afraid, Mary; you have found favor with God. You will conceive and give birth to a son, and you are to call him Jesus. He will be great and will be called the Son of the Most High. The Lord God will give him the throne of his father David, and he will reign over Jacob's descendants forever; his kingdom will never end.

~Luke 1:30-32

3

Part 1: Prisoner to the Past

Farm Life

Growing up on a farm in South Georgia in the Fifties and Sixties was difficult. Technology had not advanced enough to make farm life easier. I have the greatest respect for farmers. Numerous hours, laborious tasks, working with their hands by the sweat of their brow – no one can truly appreciate the toils of their labor unless walking a field in his/her shoes. I have. Many times.

It is a life I seldom long for, save for harvest time when vegetables come in. I love shucking corn, shelling peas and beans, canning tomatoes, making jams and jellies. I did gracious plenty of my share growing up. And I didn't mind it. I paired with Mother and would gather and prepare vegetables for cooking and/or canning and freezing. I always wished it was the only thing Mother and I had had on our list of things to do. The summer months found us rising long before the rooster crowed to get our household chores done. Then, we'd join the men in the fields.

My dad was a tobacco farmer. One of the best in the county. He grew experimental crops for different companies. He sharecropped more soil than any one person should have ever taken on. He also planted his own acreage. That was just tobacco.

There were also the multitudes of acres of corn "he" planted. *I didn't see him on the tractor nearly as much as I did my brothers.* Much was harvested, but Mother and I would shuck, scrape and freeze corn until it was time to go to grain. In addition to the corn were the vegetable gardens. The responsibility rested upon our shoulders to put away enough not only to see us through the summer months, but also until harvest the following year. The brothers would pitch in occasionally and shell beans and peas. When my baby sister was older, she assumed a role, as well. We were always grateful for any helping hands.

There were other crops. Cotton patches. Watermelon and cantaloupe fields. And then, everything would need irrigation. Miles and miles we would carry heavy irrigation pipes in order to salvage crops during frequent dry spells the South endured. My brothers were strapping hunks of pure muscle. I was lean but strong. I could "take on a grizzly," folks would say, although I never wanted to be put to that test.

Our early-morning wakeup calls found us emptying tobacco barns when each crop had been cured. The Deep South tends tobacco differently than our sister states. We put it away crop-by-crop, three to five leaves at a time, string it on a stick, hang it in a barn, and then cure it out for a week. By the time the next crop time came around, the barn had cooled down sufficiently and was ready to be unloaded and the tobacco taken to the packhouses where it was stored until auction season began later in the summer. We'd then begin unstringing the tobacco from the sticks and packing it on sheets to send it off to auction. The unstringing would take place after a long day in the field cropping the remaining leaves from the stalks. It was a vicious cycle. By the time school came around in September, farmers' kids were ready for the respite.

Mother and I would work the fields all day alongside the men. But before we could leave home in the mornings, much work had to be done. There was breakfast for a large family. *It always kept growing. After all, Dad needed an army to help run the farm.* There was also dinner (*in the South, lunch was dinner and dinner was supper*) to prepare for the family, plus the numerous laborers who were hired to help with the overabundant acreage of crops. There was seldom time to do dishes after breakfast or dinner. My hands were usually in the dishwater (*I was the dishwasher*) while Mother was getting supper ready. *My brothers occasionally pulled KP. I was ever grateful when they helped.*

After supper, I'd be back in the dishwater, and then it was time to wash the clothes. I do recall the washboards. (*No, I'm not THAT old; we were just THAT poor!*). It was a real blessing when we could afford the older wringer-type washer, even though my hands were caught in it more times than I cared for. Hanging out the jeans and khakis on the pant stretchers by moon- and/or flashlight was pretty much a nightly event. If it was a moonlit night, I got to do it alone. (*I was only afraid of the snakes; the wildcats didn't scare me nearly as much.*) I held the flashlight for Mother when it was too dark to see.

Learning Curve

I was pretty much a fearless kind of gal. Tough as whitleather. Grew up with a bunch of roughhouse boys. It was "kill or be killed" much of the time. There always seemed to be much frustration within our household. I was assigned most of the cleaning duties. That was woman's work. Cleaning up behind seven males in one small household was merciless. That accounted for much of my frustration. The boys' irritation was for other reasons, but typically had the same origin – Dad.

Living on a farm brings with it many dirty traffickers. Living on a farm with a chauvinistic father who modeled himself for six other males to follow was long-suffering. Southern sand, black rich soil, and clay. What a combination for tracking in and out of a house. My task was to try to keep it clean, and if I didn't, there would be consequences. Therefore, I took it upon myself much of the time to chase those scoundrels right out of the house and clobber them over the head with the broom if necessary. *Got a few beatings for breaking my share of the brooms.* The idea of them coming in with their work boots on and pouring out the dirt right onto the floor after I had just swept it was quite disturbing and got this gal barking. When they would laugh at me, then go right on about their business, that's when my frustration would hit the fan. I would spend much of my life as a child laboring for justice in some manner. The other would be spent simply toiling.

As exhausting as it was much of the time, I truly never begrudged the endless hours of labor on the farm, nor even the chores that encompassed them. I would learn valuable lessons about respect, compassion, kindness, gentleness, perseverance, commitment and virtue. I would come to appreciate the qualities and rewards of hard work. Taking a crop from seed to auction was a great sense of completion. Each of us would revel in the high-dollar worth of the yield. We would mourn the loss of the "child" when heavy rains or droughts claimed its merit. The farm was a tremendous learning curve. It instilled valuable work ethics within me that would serve me well throughout life, as well as my siblings.

I Was Not Alone

The farm was not the thief of my childhood. There would be exhausted memories to accompany days of tough labor. Proper rest can overcome physical exhaustion. It was the mental weariness that would imprison my heart. I was a child devoid of joy.

Oh, yes. Looking back at my childhood photos, my brown eyes sparkled with glee. A grand smile would typically cover my face. Healthy homemade curls would shine about my brow. (*Mother loved those perms, and I detested them!*) I was a picture of innocence. It is natural for children to be such. But innocence had long since betrayed me. I would not realize what was happening, but its disloyalty would initiate a process that would shackle me to a daunting past. I would begin a dark and silent private journey.

Little did I know there would be thousands upon thousands walking the same path. Indeed, I was not alone. Nor were they. But who would know? No one spoke of it. No one dared. There were signs of allies, but the darkness closed them out. Or, was it simply that everyone's eyes were closed. It's easier to dismiss if you can't see. So, I stumbled along a path with no light. It would be a lonely place. But, I had the *Word*. It would be a lamp unto my feet and a light unto my path. Where that path would lead me was yet to be revealed.

~ ~ ~

I gain understanding from your precepts;
therefore I hate every wrong path.

Your word is a lamp for my feet,
a light on my path.
I have taken an oath and confirmed it,
that I will follow your righteous laws.

~Psalm 119:104-106

> *Your past is a part of you, but it's not who you are now.*

4

Part 1: Prisoner to the Past

Memories

Your mind can protect you when no one else will. It can also become your worst enemy. I was grateful for the protection mine afforded. I have been able to block out many memories. I feel blessed for that. I have no desire to conjure up any more injustices than those I already recall, thank you. I realize that this sort of thinking runs against the grain of most every counselor you might talk to. I have never shared with a counselor. I say that not to boast. I feel certain, however, most would not have agreed with my method of not "digging up bones" in order to deal and heal. It wasn't my style. It wasn't what God had in mind for me. I did it His way. I'm glad I did.

Yes, the Great Counselor and I have had enough discussion about what I should dwell on. I can tell you this: it "ain't" the past!

This is what the LORD says—

he who made a way through the sea,

a path through the mighty waters,

who drew out the chariots and horses,

the army and reinforcements together,

and they lay there, never to rise again,

extinguished, snuffed out like a wick:

"Forget the former things;

do not dwell on the past.

See, I am doing a new thing!

Now it springs up; do you not perceive it?

I am making a way in the desert

and streams in the wasteland.

~ Isaiah 43:16-19 (NIV)

~~~

When there is constant turmoil in a home, something has to give. Little people have trouble dealing with adult stress day in and day out. When childlike eyes witness repeated atrocities of the flesh, the shock ceases to be as distressing, I suppose. The initial response might be one like mine, wherein I was frozen in time in complete disbelief of what I was seeing, hearing, and feeling. With the passing of time it converts to a run-for-cover reaction. There is fright regarding the outcome of the victim, but also fear impending personal danger. Its impairing nature can eventually block all fright of personal harm and suddenly the instinctive compassionate, protective nature kicks in. That's when assistance for the assaulted begins.

There would be many times throughout my childhood that I would block out incidents that occurred. The dysfunction that our family was going through was nothing short of an endless nightmare. My mother would become a shell of a woman going through the motions of a day. She would stay pregnant and working, whether in the fields or at home, until the minute each child was born. (*I was the first to be born in the hospital. The older two boys were born at home.*) She would also be abused at every level during her pregnancy. How she ever kept her babies in the womb without harm to them is miraculous, indeed. God's hedge of protection certainly encompassed her during each pregnancy. None of us children was disabled or had a birth defect in any manner. That is amazing!

I was grateful when Mother went against my dad's wishes, at high cost I might add, and took measures for birth control. His intent was for her to bear his army to work on the farm. She stopped at eight. Her health would probably have not seen her through another. Nor was she emotionally stable enough to handle the ones who already needed care.

Mother would resort to the use of alcohol, which was introduced and at times forced to drink by our father. She abused prescription drugs for many years in an attempt to cope with life and its difficulties. Perfunctorily performing her duties, she became devoid of emotion until her anger became uncontrollable. It was during these times she became our greatest challenge in a day. I, for one, was grateful her anger was infrequent. Having to avoid striking blows from both parents was physically and emotionally difficult to balance.

I would become a surrogate mother to the four youngest of my siblings. Mother was emotionally shattered and physically drained. She got by on very little sleep. Her long list of household responsibilities were interrupted by verbal, physical and sexual assaults. The house was too small for incidents to go unnoticed by all occupants.

What time she wasn't laboring for my dad or being abused by him, she was pining over his misspent actions while away from home. She spent the few hours she had to herself stewing over him being out drinking with his cronies. Some of them were a bit more "dearish" than others. She was keenly aware of his shenanigans by the evidence left on his clothes. He was never a good liar. His body language gave him up. No eye contact. A sheepish grin. Walking away to avoid discussion. A flush would come over his very ruddy complexion. His giddiness over his misbehavior was insulting.

~~~

The kind of betrayal adultery inflicts to a woman's heart is insufferable. What draws a woman to a man who is not only an abuser physically, but emotionally as well? How do you step out of love once you fall into it? The connection has been made. The flesh-to-flesh union is solidifying. Commitment is in place. Or, should be. Today's world steps to a different beat. We test the water before making a commitment. We don't even like the word anymore. It's become an option in many circles, but especially in matters of love. Interesting concept, especially in light of the fact that God's word hasn't changed regarding the intent of this kind of union.

~~~

Wives, submit yourselves to your own husbands as you do to the Lord. For the husband is the head of the wife as Christ is the head of the church, his body, of which he is the Savior. Now as the church submits to Christ, so also wives should submit to their husbands in everything. Husbands, love your wives, just as Christ loved the church and gave himself up for her to make her holy, cleansing her by the washing with water through the word, and to present her to himself as a radiant church, without stain or wrinkle or any other blemish, but holy and blameless. In this same way, husbands ought to love their wives as their own bodies. He who loves his wife loves himself. After all, no one ever hated their own body, but they feed and care for their body, just as Christ does the church— for we are members of his body. "For this reason a man will leave his father and mother and be united to his wife, and the two will become one flesh." This is a profound mystery—but I am talking about Christ and the church. However, each one of you also must love his wife as he loves himself, and the wife must respect her husband.   ~Ephesians 5:21-33 (NIV)

~~~

But for those who have made a commitment, He gives people an out. He made provisions for misuse of this covenant relationship because He knew man's heart. He knew there would be need for such a proviso. What keeps a woman – or man – in an environment of abuse of this process of marriage? The heart is so vulnerable to pain under the throes of infidelity. The agony is so severe that you scarce recognize yourself and why you exist. You want to stop the world and just get off at the next train bound for anywhere.

It must be akin to Sherman's march on Atlanta where he set ablaze a part of history that can never be recovered. To the victim of the blaze, it's debilitating. Everything ceases to matter. Life has no meaning. It's devoid of purpose. Everything you've invested in, you've worked for, and you've dreamed of has gone up in smoke. The devastation it leaves behind will take years to rebuild. If ever.

The domino effect is perhaps more damaging. Why exist in a relationship where there is constant abuse? Whether you're the victim or the assailant, whether the abuse is verbal, physical, sexual and/or adulterous, the message it sends to the innocent children (and others) is that the behavior is acceptable. So, we put our blessing on our children being treated by or treating someone else in like manner. And the "beat" goes on.

~~~

Prime Targets

Vivid pictures course my mind of Mother sitting on the front porch smoking her cigarettes in an act of defiance. She was forbidden to smoke by my father. Her blatant but secret disregard for his wishes was remanded to the open air. Had she smoked inside, the scent would have become an olfactory betrayal. He would have then used smoking as the excuse for the beating she would receive when he got home. There was sure one to come. Excuse wasn't necessarily a prerequisite.

Dad was a honky-tonker. He was a charmer. He exhibited a great personality to everyone but his family. He stood about six-foot-two. Striking features. Indian bloodline. Stark black hair. Strong cheekbones. Ruddy complexion. A real looker. And, he had talent. I suppose one would call it that. He could play a guitar and carry a tune. I always felt he was far too restrained in vocal volume. I likened it to lack of self-confidence. I felt he deserved that deficit in character. But, then again, I also knew that was part of his assertion for power over a woman.

All these qualities Dad possessed – the good and bad – acted as a magnet for women. My recollection is he always had someone he was seeing on the side. Or, two or three. Only one brief stint had he given up his weakness in the flesh. I was elated. We all were. We caught a glimpse of what real life on a farm could have been, but it was short-lived. *We'll talk more about that later.*

His lack of self-confidence was definitely a stumbling block for him. Tales of the family say we have his father to thank for that. Dad would attempt to overshadow his weaknesses by bullying his wife and kids. I suppose that appeased a forgotten spirit within him.

~~~

Funny thing; men who beat up on women are frustrated over lack of power. Their forceful nature, when used correctly, could be channeled into positive avenues. Yet, they choose to inflict their vents of anger upon weak, fragile, delicate women. When the woman is so beaten down she's unconscious, her best hope is that he'll be too exhausted or too intoxicated to go after the children.

~~~

We were weak and fragile. Prime targets. Dad wasn't always too tired or too drunk. We were happy if he was both. The drunkenness was almost always a given; not his exhaustion.

~~~

Men like my dad are pathetic representations of their gender. Their example becomes a family trademark. Their sons typically follow the same course and will go through an assortment of women trying to find one who will hang with them for the long haul. Funny thing, not all women reject being abused. Many daughters who have witnessed their mother being abused are drawn to men who abuse.

42

Today, there are many programs available which have been designed to aid victims of abuse. In my experience in the legal industry as well as the ministry my husband and I share, I see many women who choose to live in the abuse. For many of them, their self-worth has been stripped away and they feel they deserve what they get in the way of abuse. Some of them have nowhere else to go after the government assistance runs out. Others are madly in love with "Nothing," so they stay with him.

And so the cycle goes. And on and on and on. Until someone breaks the sadistic sequence.

~~~

For you were once darkness, but now you are light in the Lord. Live as children of light (for the fruit of the light consists in all goodness, righteousness and truth) and find out what pleases the Lord. Have nothing to do with the fruitless deeds of darkness, but rather expose them. For it is shameful even to mention what the disobedient do in secret. But everything exposed by the light becomes visible, for it is light that makes everything visible. This is why it is said: "Wake up, O sleeper, rise from the dead, and Christ will shine on you." Be very careful, then, how you live—not as unwise but as wise, making the most of every opportunity, because the days are evil. Therefore do not be foolish, but understand what the Lord's will is.

~Ephesians 5:8-17 (NIV)

People will hurt you again, but your contentment in those times of heartache will measure differently from before.

5

Part 1: Prisoner to the Past

Chosen Memories

I kept my memories at bay. I was in the mode of survival. Memories made me fitful; I chose the fittest. If there was no benefit in the memory, I discarded it. Why hang onto something hurtful, a memory where I would take away nothing but pain? It was pointless. It served no purpose and only broke me down. If there would be a lesson, then it would be worth revisiting. Otherwise, it was over. Done. Move on.

School was a safe haven. I was not exposed to any other place outside of home other than my grandparents' homes, and those visits were infrequent for both sets of grands. Education was becoming my friend, my soulmate, and my awareness that there could be another way to live. I would learn to love the months attending school.

When one is suppressed at home, he/she looks for avenues of expression in other areas. School was my expectation of release. I never lost hope for each day to be the turn-around point in my life. I anticipated some teacher – any teacher – to look at me with compassionate eyes, to reach out with a genuine concern to make me feel special, and overlook my tattered, worn look. That would not happen for many years. Elementary and junior high school were no fun at all. High school was better, but still a stretch at best. By that time, I had honed to a real science the art of masking emotions.

Day after day I longed to be "special." My heart's desire was to feel I had significance for being there. Time and again I would leave despondent; a sense of rejection weighing heavy within. Not accepted. I was funny, but not funny enough. I was smart, but not smart enough. I was friendly, but no one befriended me. It was a lonely place of refuge, but someone in my position would take whatever safe haven she found.

My anxious heart waited for the lot to fall to me to be the teacher's helper. I wanted to be like Melanie. From grammar school forward, Melanie was always the fair-haired assistant. Why wouldn't she be? She was beautiful. Her blonde hair fell lavishly upon her shoulders. Her bright, blue eyes glistened without worry. Her complexion was flawless. High cheekbones. Confident smile. Perfect poise. Dressed to the nines. Her world was perfect. Or, so it appeared. There was a confidence in her gait as she proudly fulfilled her assigned task from the teacher and made deliveries to the school office. There would be others who were among the chosen to assume responsibilities, and each executed them with an appropriate I-am-special display of pride.

As I grew, so did my desire to be like everyone else. Even as an elementary school child, that sense of belonging, of being set apart and singled out as worthy, would swell up until I felt I would burst in a pool of tears. Should I do so, I was quite certain I would be embarrassed as the teacher would hush me up, stand me in a corner until I could regain my composure, or put me out in the hallway to make a spectacle and compound the whole emotional scene. It was the lack of concern for why one would behave with such regard that left the heart more broken than when the breakdown began. There would be only one such occasion for me. I was much younger. That would never happen again. The dam might break inside, but it would be a silent drowning in my heart. No one else would be invited to my flood.

Forgotten Teen

Introduction into teenhood can be an exciting time. It was no less exciting for me. What was going on in my home did not deter my inherent process of emergence. It only squelched the activities associated with the ensuing development. High school devoid of activities can find one floundering and/or going through the motions of trying to fit in with classmates.

Study hall time would never be a social hour for me. I feverishly rushed through homework knowing there would be no opportunity at home to complete it. The cute, popular girls sat atop their desks in flirtatious fashion. The boys gathered around engaged in laughter as they clicked off stories designed to amuse and impress their targeted pursuits. The hour was a fast one, and all of us were sorry to see it end. The friends' circle catch-up hour would come to an abrupt end. I would gather my books, put away homework, and assess what would have to be finished on the bus ride home that afternoon. Particularly heavy assignments oftentimes found me finishing homework after midnight – after all the chores were done and everyone was fast asleep – except for my poor mother who was usually being beaten and/or ravished by my dad. *(And yes, some husbands do rape their wives.)* The new addition to our home still kept us in tight quarters. Doors were not soundproof, and locks were easily picked.

I busied myself at school. I tried to make friends, but they seemed to keep their distance. I was a pleasant person. Quite the little chatterbox, actually. There was much to say. I never really talked much at home. Not meaningful talk, anyway. I squawked at my brothers incessantly. We were always getting underneath one another's skin about something. Usually it was over my cleaning and their messing up. So, to be able to have conversations at school was refreshing, when I found a tolerate ear.

Hallmark Memories

Ms. Williams, my first-grade teacher, was a remarkable lady, I had surmised. She never appeared to be sad; just stern. She never looked tired, although, she didn't seem to have to work as hard as my mom. She always dressed nicely. She was kind to me. It was a welcome alteration to my life. I didn't dress like everyone else. That was quite obvious. She didn't seem to mind that much. But, she did seat me in the back of the room. *I didn't understand why for a long time. That revelation would come later on.* I always wanted to sit up front, but that seemed to be reserved for the "city" kids. We were farmers. We had our place. (*Trust me, anyone would laugh to think of Lakeland, Georgia as a "city." Then or now.*)

I didn't mind first-grade memories much. At first, that is. Later that year I would begin to set aside points of reference in my life. There are some memories you can't dislodge because you shouldn't. They're the hallmark memories, the ones that forge through your life with great energy. These memories determine your strength. They set the pace for greatness or defeat. These recollections speak of your value. They shape resolve. They offer hope. These are the memories you use to remind yourself you *are* someone special. And what you do with those memories – those gentle reminders of a past for which you had no control – will define your destiny. A few years later, I would learn the art of ensnaring only those who had significant meaning. The others would find another place to inhabit. I could not allow them to set up residence in my mind if I were to function day to day. I would soon discover the means of survival of the fittest.

~~~

Therefore, since we are surrounded by such a great cloud of witnesses, let us throw off everything that hinders and the sin that so easily entangles. And let us run with perseverance the race marked out for us, fixing our eyes on Jesus, the pioneer and perfecter of faith. For the joy set before him he endured the cross, scorning its shame, and sat down at the right hand of the throne of God. Consider him who endured such opposition from sinners, so that you will not grow weary and lose heart.

~Hebrews 12:1-3

> *Impatience can be a stumbling block in adverse situations.*

6

Part 1: Prisoner to the Past

Someone is Hurting Your Little Girl

It was my first year in school. The initial memory I have as a young girl is not one I would wish upon my worst enemy. I found myself sitting in a doctor's office with my mother. I really knew nothing of the meaning of the words being exchanged between them. But, I distinctly recall the white-haired doctor telling my mother, "Lola, this isn't right. Someone is hurting your little girl, and you've got to take care of it." I can remember the look on my mother's face being one of sadness. Not shock. Not concern. Not anger, nor even fear. Just sadness.

I was confused by what I was hearing. I knew she had taken me in because I had come to her with blood on my panties, crying that I was hurting. She took me in to see Dr. Phillips, and as we drove there, she explained to me that I was probably starting some "cycle." She never asked me how I got hurt or who hurt me. I was five years old – a first-grader. I knew nothing of what she was talking about. I just knew I was sore, confused and needed my mother to take care of things for me. She responded with silence. Not a word was ever spoken to me about it again. She would never question me as to who hurt me, she would never inquire if I was continuing to get hurt, and she would never, ever know how much I would resent her silence for years to come.

~~~

Approximately a year before her death, Mother did ask me if I had ever been "bothered by my father." Now, bothered is Southern terminology for "molested." There's also another term that is familiar in the South – "messed with." Everyone knew to stay away from that expression. It's much like how trendy idioms come to have different connotations these days. For instance, we can no longer say the words "hooked up" or "connected." There was a time that "gay" meant happy and "queen" meant royalty. We must be careful, Little Tongues, how we say things. Words take on a whole new meaning. It's more than semantics; it's labeling.

The violation that occurs to a child is irrevocable. The harm immeasurable. Repeated offenses become insurmountable. To say the damage had been done would minimize its repulsive nature. It is one of the most heinous crimes known to man.

What's that? What did I say to my mom? What could I say? I simply told her, "Mother, that's all in the past. It doesn't matter one way or the other any longer. It's all water over the dam. Don't worry yourself over something you can't change even though it needed to be. Jesus has that under control." And that was that.

7

Part 1: Prisoner to the Past

The End of Warmth

It would be the following year that I would hang onto my next childhood memory – that of my mother's parents coming to her defense. Now, Granddaddy Noles was my hero. He was a little, wiry man, about five-foot-three. I was the apple of his eye, as was my mother – his only girl. By this point, he was the only male in my life I trusted not to hurt me.

He played piano by ear. The natural ability was an incredible talent to me. How I longed to play. I knew he hoped I would develop the natural gift. It must have been a disappointment to him when I didn't. But I could sing. I could carry a tune and wasn't shy about shouting it out. *That reserve would come later.* So, I would sit in his lap and sing as he played. I would sing, "Jesus Loves Me" and "This Old Man" and "Old Man River." Those were good memories, truly good times. I can still feel the warmth of my Granddaddy's touch as he would place his arthritic-ridden fingers on my hand and set them atop the keyboard. Memorizing the chords to be played was not what he wanted. He wanted me to feel the rhythm, to sense the cadence, to adopt the natural ear for playing. In hindsight, I believe he must have been praying over me to receive that gift as he guided my hands. I cherish those moments with him.

~~~

I would inherit that piano once Granddaddy's arthritis prohibited him from playing. He and my uncle loaded it up on a truck and brought it to my house. He told my mother he was going to pay for me to have lessons. (Since I didn't inherit the natural talent.) I was thrilled, but my father, not so much. As soon as he walked in the door and saw the gift from Granddaddy, there were no questions asked. He rolled that piano to the doorway, and then shoved it into the yard, bursting it into a hundred pieces. I cried a river that day. I was broken-hearted over the loss of the chance to do something special in my life, and for the loss of the warmth that piano brought me. I actually did take up piano later in life in honor of my granddaddy. Life was just too packed to keep it up, however. Pregnant with my first child and very sick, working a full-time job, going to college at night, and Webby – the hubby – being away from home at seminary was too much for even me. I've threatened to get back to it someday. I owe it to Granddaddy, and myself.)

~~~

Nannie (*Not Nana, but Nannie and not Nanny, like a hired custodian of children, but Nannie*) was patient to listen to Granddaddy and me. She would eventually become overwrought with the bellowing and call a halt to end our good time. Granddaddy would close up the keyboard and move on to other things to entertain me, like walking through his small vineyard picking grapes or plucking Catawba worms for fishing.

Granddaddy was special to me. He was a quiet spirit with a soft, hearty laugh. Kind. Gentle. He possessed a tender love for his children and grands. Those traits are rare, you know. My mother had his nature. I'm sure it was there all along, but life had hardened her and these qualities became repressed. That nature surfaced again after her divorce from my father after 32 years, and especially was evident in the last years of her life.

Beginning of a Desolate Season

My grandparents were foster parents, as well, and their home was a tender place for uprooted children to heal. What a shock it must have been to my mother's system for her to transition from the heavenly to the hellish!

I would learn at some point that Dad had beaten Mother within the first two weeks of their marriage. But then, in 1947, you made your bed and you laid in it. You didn't run back to mommy and daddy. There wasn't a 1-800 number or Shelter House to fall back on, and the law enforcement operated like some of the agencies do even today – they stuck by the "good ol' boys."

The night of this second hallmark memory, my mother had been beaten beyond recognition. We didn't have a phone yet. We were the last to get many things. Multiple children in the family kept us as poor as church mice – and looked down upon in the community. That night was a worse-than-usual scene. All of us kids were screaming and kicking, begging and pleading for Dad to stop. We were pretty battered ourselves before the end of the whole ordeal. One of the neighbors had heard all that was going on. He was no better off than us financially, and calling was out of the question, so he drove into town to retrieve my granddad.

Granddaddy and Nannie hurried out to the homeplace and tried to help. The dust had just begun to settle on the free-for-all event, but it soon kicked back up again. They tried to take Mother and, at this time, the five children with them. When they did, Dad turned on the two of them, inflicting injury and a chasm between the families. It is a scene I am confident will never be erased from my memory. My father's tall stature loomed over the docile frame of my grandfather, beating him madly and relentlessly.

My grandmother stepped in to pull him off and my father belted her in the stomach and face. She was a sizable woman, yet he threw her around as thought she was a feather. It was a horrific sight. My heart was rent watching the man I adored being battered. We were all defenseless to Dad's strength in times of anger. His temper would override any mindful thoughts, and his conscience was becoming numb to remorse.

My grandparents gathered up their pride and dignity and implored their daughter to get in the car. Mother was afraid to leave. I can only surmise her fear rested in the fact that he would hurt them even worse. He had guns. We had seen them before. Most of us kids were crying and begging to go. Instead, we remained prisoners in the household to witness and suffer injury for many years to come. My grandparents never set foot in our home again, and we were forbidden to see them for several years. It was a desolate season in this little girl's life without the warmth from my grandfather. I know I was always in his heart, and his lips uttered many prayers on my behalf.

~~~

> But you, Sovereign LORD,
> help me for your name's sake;
> out of the goodness of your love, deliver me.
> For I am poor and needy,
> and my heart is wounded within me.
> I fade away like an evening shadow;
> I am shaken off like a locust.
>
> ~Psalm 109:21-23 (NIV)

8

Part 1: Prisoner to the Past

The Promise

Most of us would give our right arm *(relax, it's just one of those semantic things)* for five or ten years off our age. Especially women. While I would be grateful to claim that youth, I will stay right where I am. Three years later in the course of history might have altered the turning point for my life. There's no bargaining for me.

In early 1960, I was almost eight years old. *(I spoke of this earlier in the introduction, but since many readers don't do those, I'll give a recap with a bit more detail.)* That was the same year Madalyn Murray O'Hair filed the lawsuit that would change the course of America. Her lone voice would be heard by the Supreme Court in 1963 and echo throughout our country, overriding the slumbering voices of Christians. It would forever alter the means to reach those like myself on a path devoid of Light. *We have gained some ground throughout the course of years regarding groups being allowed to meet and pray in schools, but we have lost many battles as well. In fact, we continue to lose our position in many areas. Our voices are strong, but we cannot be timid about sounding our cause!*

The Gideons came to our school and spoke at chapel (*as we called it; assembly for others*). They did this every year, but I got to hear them this time. They were giving out the tiny red Biblettes, if you will, that had the familiar verses of John 3:16, Psalm 100, and a few other passages of scripture. They presented the gospel of Jesus Christ to the group, and these little eager ears didn't let a single word go unrecorded. My short legs raced up to the front of the room and claimed the Bible they offered to those who wanted a "real" one. As I mentioned, that Gideons' Bible would be read underneath my covers by flashlight.

Grasping Solace

In the very beginning, my young mind couldn't comprehend and piece together the complexities of some of its teaching. Much of it was gibberish because of my meager vocabulary and understanding. I certainly understood the part about "For God so loved the world" – and that world was "me." Now, *that* I could apply to my life. And I also could relate to the part, "Come unto me, all ye who are weary and heavy-laden, and I will give you rest." The *rest* part really registered, because everyone in our household needed that break.

That Gideons' Bible would be my solace, reading it until I fell asleep at night … or being interrupted by an intruder after the lights went out. As I matured in knowledge, I began grasping more and more of God's promises. That was when I cranked up on the book of Philippians. Ephesians was melting me down, too. This stuff was revealing!

The Homeplace

The winter months found me spending more time reading. The grueling summer burdens shortened the opportunity. The exit leading out to the back porch area was the exact size for a foldout cot to slide in, protruding into the hallway about six inches. There was no privacy. There was no room. I climbed over the rails at the head of the bed to enter and exit my bed. Until that time, I had stayed in the room next to that hallway with all the boys. *(Yeah, not a great scenario. The new setup was a really lame attempt to get me out of a bad situation.)* Our four-room home was a matchbox originally: a small kitchen, dining area, a living room, and one bedroom for all the kids. Mother, Dad and whatever new baby was on the scene at the time occupied the dining room. We all ate around a small kitchen table. The boys sat; the girls stood. We didn't have a bathroom for many years. *Yep, one of them there outhouses. Stop that! I told you I'm not that old; we were just that poor.*

We did eventually get a bathroom added, which created the alcove area for my "bedroom." The bath area was a welcomed arrival to the household! Once we finally acquired one, the wringer washer was positioned on the back porch. Brrrr, it made for some cold wintertime laundry days, which was every day in a big household, but Mother and I were ever so grateful not to have to scrub on the washboard. We always hung our clothes on the clothesline, rain or shine. We also had our big chest-type freezers on the porch. Once they were filled, the crops were about over and done, and so were Mother and I. It was a *passel of work*, as we used to say in the South.

Dad was a carpenter by trade during the spring, fall and winter months. He must've been very good at what he did. His sons learned the trade by hard knocks and became masters of woodworking. They have been blessed to provide for their families with these skills. Aside from gardens, none of them remained farmers. That fact, alone, speaks volumes for how hard we all worked. Typically, the carpentry jobs would bleed over into the tobacco harvesting time, and that made it especially difficult on everyone trying to keep the balance between paying the bills and not letting the crops go to seed.

There's some truth to the tale that whatever a person's trade, you can bet their homes are in desperate need of their services. It was the gospel at the carpenter's house I grew up in. But, Dad would finally add on three more small bedrooms and an additional bath. And while he was at it, he bricked the home so it no longer looked like a shack. The community was happy to see the exterior facelift. Little did they know (*although, their knowledge is a debatable issue with me, still*) the interior was still in shambles. It was business as usual. The saga of our lives would never change one iota.

I kept to task, reading my Gideons' Bible. It would continue to nourish my spirit. I would not understand many of its promises quite yet, but my heart would resonate with the words of Philippians 4:8 ... *whatever is true, noble, right, pure, lovely, admirable, excellent or praiseworthy.* I would think about such things while getting past the past.

9

Part 1: Prisoner to the Past

Mantel Prayer

I can remember the moment I adopted that Philippians verse as my sustaining promise. I was ten by then. Crop failure the prior summer had strapped us even more than usual. It was Saturday. Mother was working outside the home to bring in extra money, and that left me with the major responsibilities of the house. It had been a really difficult Friday night for me. I was exhausted from little sleep, much abuse, and I felt emotionally busted.

The day began with me burning breakfast and getting a good thrashing for having done so. I was charged with cleaning the house and watching the babies while everyone else had gone uptown to the movies, or wherever the boys would gallivant. Babies were down for naps, and I began to clean up after the others. I felt desperately alone, dreadfully forsaken, and completely desolate.

A Cinderella Moment

I typically relished those quiet moments. They were few and far between. It was time alone, save for the toddlers and baby. They were asleep at the time, and it was just me and the sound of the swooshing broom against the linoleum flooring in the one bedroom that housed all of us kids.

We'd had burned logs in the fireplace earlier that morning. It was our only source of warmth. Its dual purpose fronted the living area on the other side of the wall. Any debris I gathered would be swept into the fireplace along with the ashes. I'd dump them later and get it ready for the next morning's blaze. It was a Cinderella moment as I dragged the broom across the floor. I picked up shoes and clothes and had already washed, wrung, and line-dried several loads of laundry. I had ironed clothes everyone would need for the day. Saturday dinner had been served up, dishes done. I had swept and mopped the kitchen, living area and room where Mother and Daddy slept. I'd changed the linens in the baby's bed and washed and folded my baby sister's clothes and diapers.

If I had enough time in the day, I would make her another dress. We had a couple of pretty calico flour sacks from the week's groceries, and it was just enough to whip up a pretty little frock for her. I was fortunate to have picked up the interest to sew before we were no longer permitted to go to Nannie's. She had shown me the art of being a seamstress on her nifty Singer sewing machine. I made nearly everything my baby sister and I wore. It was a skill I treasured.

~~~

I loved being productive. Even then. No time for daydreaming. I didn't even know how. I enjoyed reading, but stolen moments were precious few. School was the sole provider of my bent for knowledge. If dreaming were allowed amidst being charged as caretaker of the home, it would have been to steal away with Twain's The Adventures of Huckleberry Finn, *or Stowe's* Uncle Tom's Cabin. *As I grew in maturity and appreciation of literature, I discovered Hawthorne's* The Scarlet Letter, London's The Call of the Wild, *and Dickens'* A Tale of Two Cities. *Being mandatory in school was my only hope of saturating myself with these classics. Oh, to be able to sit and read at leisure. How inviting the sound!*

~~~

An Unwanted Friend

But today, the silence invited the anguish from within to spill forth. It was a day the prison walls closed in on me. I was coming into the knowledge of how wretched my life really was. School brought much of the information I would learn about the world. I was exposed to worldly things children should never be burdened with in my home.

My heart was heavy that week. It was the anatomy class at school for fifth-graders. It was the time for young girls to be visited by their "friend." For fear it may not be broached at home by moms, the school felt it incumbent to teach girls about the menstrual cycle and the trials and prevails that accompany this newfound experience.

I recall the girls in class being giddy. Some bragged about *their* "friend" coming early, so they found the film boring. Others were intrigued and excited to be introduced to this new development. As the story unfolded, I sat petrified. I was horrified at what I was learning about the imminent direction of my life.

My thoughts raced back to the film again, and the sweeping ceased. I propped the broom against the wall, cradled my head in the crook of my arm as I rested it on the mantel, and I began to sob. The wellspring that poured forth had been bottled up for too long. I cried out to God with great agony in my plea. "Lord, if you hear me, get me out of this mess! Why do you leave me here? Just take my life. To die would be better than this."

I would scream and shake my fist at the Lord in great anger because He was denying me passage to freedom. I wanted so much to be like the Job man I had read about. I wanted to be someone who could stand every trial that came my way. But, I was just a little girl. Why wouldn't someone help me?

~~~

My anger didn't stop at God. I was angry at the world for not caring. No teacher, no counselor, no neighbor, no friend…no one would open his or her eyes wide enough to recognize the signs people wear when they're being abused in some manner. They're so obvious. Yet, the blind eye and deaf ear would be the excuse they would harbor. Every child needs an advocate – a voice to speak on his/her behalf. Children are powerless against the whim of adults. And even, at times, defenseless against other kids. I was a kid being abused by kids who had been taught by adults how to abuse.

It was an insane place to live – this halfway-house prison. I could come and go, not as I pleased, but I certainly was not chained to any wall or post. I wasn't shackled at the ankles and tortured like many stories you hear of abused children. But, a child can't reconcile in the heart and mind of stepping outside of a parent's care, out of the home that should be secure, a safe haven, and a refuge. The desire to be loved and accepted by one's parents is a strong force. It is the natural course of life.

It is peculiar, isn't it? A child knows that sexual molestation in any form, from anyone, is just not right. Born innocent into a world of perversion, a child innately knows when a touch is forbidden. And then, fear is so easily instilled in a child. Children are so trusting that you can tell them anything, and they will believe it is the truth. Vulnerable. Delicate. Innocent. Too often tainted by the world.

I simply needed someone, anyone to care. Someone who would recognize that the repetition of visible bruising and stripes was abnormal. Someone to identify the hollowness in my eyes, the gaunt look in my face, the nervous behavior I exhibited. I desired someone to be familiar with the need, the longing in my voice and countenance for attention, for love, for life. It was obvious. I did everything but tell them, "Please rescue me!" No one read between the lines. No one attached emotionally to me. It was family business, and no one would cross those boundaries.

Why? Was it too risky? Was it too much trouble? Was it fear of the unknown? Was it that they might be wrong and feel embarrassed to have thought such a horrible thing about this family? What could have kept an adult in a responsible position from rescuing a child from this kind of exploitation? Even if someone didn't suspect the sexual abuse, the physical would have been enough to blow a whistle. Yet, no one came with a key to unlock the door to my silent prison. I would go back day after day to the halfway house, behind four walls of jail hell, and try to cope as best I could as a child in a sick and sordid world.

If you know someone you suspect is being abused – the hidden abuse, silent abuse, don't wait to be told. It probably won't happen. If you are a mother being abused, or you suspect your child may be, become an advocate. Get to safety. A child fears he/she won't be believed. And if not believed, going back into the situation is even worse, especially when it is investigated and unproven. Please, be his/her advocate. Read between the lines. Many just want it to be discovered without having to tell. The guilt of selling out one's family is a heavy burden. Most children will not do this, because family is, or should be, sacred. Don't assume you can't help. Children need to be rescued. When no one comes to a child's defense, life can get very complicated. I was lucky to be a survivor. Many aren't.

~~~

Defining Moment

My mantel prayer would be a defining moment in my childhood. When I had screamed until I couldn't, I fell to the floor, begging for mercy, and cradling myself, rocking back and forth, back and forth. Weeping. Cleansing. Releasing brokenness. I began reciting my banner verse ... *whatever is true, whatever is noble, whatever is right, whatever is pure, whatever is lovely, whatever is admirable—if anything is excellent or praiseworthy—think about such things.*

Peace began to envelope me, and I would sense a calm I had never experienced. It was as though God's hand stretched from His throne and rested upon my very shoulders that day. I promised Him if He would help me survive what was happening to me, if He could just protect my body, if He would get me out of this mess, I would serve Him forever. I didn't know how He would do it, but I knew it was within His power. "I know you are a God who can do everything. I've read about your miracles. Please make one happen for me, Dear Lord. Please, just love me enough to protect me. "

Memory Mixed With an Emotion

I would plead with God that my prayer went beyond the ceiling and didn't get trapped within the pine walls of that awful house. That day I would cry until the well ran dry. I promised God if He would help me, I would never cry again. *He knew that was an unrealistic pledge, but I have managed to limit my tears through the years.* It was a memory mixed with emotion. When I arose, it was with the strength of the Lord. His assurance was breathed on me at the moment I felt His presence. It would be my first real experience of a promise from God. My spirit was convicted.

Did I understand what was happening as a child? I'm uncertain. I do know that I felt a change. I experienced a sense of peace invade me down to my very toes. I was no longer fighting the battle alone. There would be intervention. I didn't know how. I didn't know whom. I rested in calm assurance there would be protection. And that was that. *And protect me He did. I would not get my "friend" until I was a senior in high school – about two months before I graduated. I was 17 years old. Truly a miracle of protection.*

The rest of that day and others brought new challenges, but I would focus on the true, the noble, the pure and lovely. And the odd thing was, I didn't even know what those things were. I just knew whatever they might be had to be better than what I was accustomed.

~~~

> The LORD is King forever and ever; the nations will perish from his land. You hear, O LORD, the desire of the afflicted; you encourage them, and you listen to their cry, defending the fatherless and the oppressed, in order that man, who is of the earth, may terrify no more.
> ~Psalm 10:16-18 (NIV)

~~~

10
Part 1: Prisoner to the Past

Sunrise Love

It would be shortly after that outcry that I would make arrangements with a neighboring farmer's family for a ride to their church. My dad, being the hellion preacher's kid, apparently was in some state of rebellion against the church. I wish I knew the circumstances surrounding his childhood. My heart was heavy for him much of the time. He, obviously, had his own demons to deal with. Then, the world got hold of him. It was too tempting. It offered too much pleasure. His foundation was too weak to overcome. But, here again, I've seen some very strong foundations crumble from the pleasures of the world.

~~~

Don't you know people like that? Once the flesh tastes the forbidden fruit, a wildfire is set loose in their soul. It's inextinguishable. It burns so deeply that all feeling of guilt is lost. Justification sets in. Then ownership. Once people believe they have the right to act a certain way, no longer is their behavior an abomination against mankind, nor the Lord. The vortex of sin creates spirals round and round until everyone who has personal association with the fallen person is sucked into all consequences. Some people fight desperately to pull themselves out of the whirlpool of hurt; others merely get drawn into its pit of despair.

In desperate search of something to cure their souls ravaged by the wildfire, they furiously seek. Who will help them once bridges with family and friends have been burned? Who will care should they get a healthy portion of just deserves? Who will call them by name and drag them from their brokenness of life?

~~~

I will exalt you, O Lord, for you lifted me out of the depths and did not let my enemies gloat over me. O LORD my God, I called to you for help and you healed me. O LORD, you brought me up from the grave; you spared me from going down into the pit. Sing to the LORD, you saints of his; praise his holy name. For his anger lasts only a moment, but his favor lasts a lifetime; weeping may remain for a night, but rejoicing comes in the morning. When I felt secure, I said, "I will never be shaken." O Lord, when you favored me, you made my mountain stand firm; but when you hid your face, I was dismayed. To you, O Lord, I called; to the Lord I cried for mercy: "What gain is there in my destruction, in my going down into the pit? Will the dust praise you? Will it proclaim your faithfulness? Hear, O Lord, and be

> merciful to me; O Lord, be my help." You turned my wailing into dancing; you removed my sackcloth and clothed me with joy, that my heart may sing to you and not be silent. O Lord my God, I will give you thanks forever.
>
> ~Psalm 30 (NIV)

~~~

All in the Family

My Granddaddy Suggs was a Primitive Baptist preacher. Out of deference to his father, and perhaps a wee bit of regard for his belief in a Higher Power, my dad would manage to grace church with his presence on Homecoming Sunday and again on Easter. Funny, I never recall attending a single Christmas service as a small child. Dad was usually on a drunken binge 'round about that time, which made Christmases at our household pretty unpleasant.

My scattered memories of church experiences are most likely attributed to the fact my herpetophobia swept over me. I would close my eyes and intentionally block out some of the events going on inside the church building. I did manage to retain images of the foot-washing ceremony that would take place each time.

~~~

For a few years, I attributed my obedience to my dad's demand that I wash every male's feet in the household that would eventually be seven — yes, seven males, fourteen feet — as being obedient to God. As I grew older and began vocalizing my perceptions, my father and I would have, shall we call it, "heated debates" regarding his lack of obedience in other areas of his life concerning God's expectations of me. I realized this washing-the-feet ritual was in actuality merely another facet of his male chauvinism. That notion didn't go over too well with me even as a young, impressionable girl. I ultimately won that battle.

~~~

Granddaddy was enthusiastic and passionate in the pulpit. He could bellow out hellfire and brimstone with the best of them. The old country church was set back off a beaten path. (*I couldn't take you there today if you stuck a gun to my head!*). Homecoming was complete with dinner on the grounds, and in the South, that spells *Paula Deen* kind of specialties!

Easter was my favorite day, though. I can recall being uninformed of its whole intent initially. The only meaning it held for me was "frockin' up" and looking pretty. My mother did her best to pull a feeble production out of her rat-stash for every child for Easter. I could hardly wait to don my little lace gloves, new patent leather shoes with ruffled-edged socks, and the fancy dress complete with crinoline! We were all spit-shined, polished, and expected to be on our best behavior. I felt very special that day. It was a day I came to anticipate each year.

~~~

Our Easter celebration at home would begin a bit earlier in the week. I recall poking holes in the ends of the eggs and blowing out their innards. There was a real art to that feat. I recall the self-induced headache until I perfected the skill. Initially, Mother would laugh at the broken egg all in my hands, but soon worked up to a good scolding if it happened too often. When enough eggs had been blown clean, I would dye the empty shells, let them dry, rig a ribbon through the hole, then tie them on a Dogwood limb full of blooms. They were gorgeous amidst the array of white and pink splendor of flowers. The display graced our dinner table, and I recall being especially proud of my creative depiction of Easter.

The Easter bunny didn't hop to our front door and bring us baskets of goodies as he did for my kids and now my grands. We did, however, hard-boil and dye eggs and have an egg hunt on Saturday afternoon, since the bulk of our day on Sunday was spent at church. Mother always made certain there was a prize egg. It was never anything big – usually a marshmallow bunny. The biggest thrill of the treasure was simply being the one to lay claim to the find.

I can remember yet another favorite part of the Easter tradition was the baby chicks. Part of our farm profits consisted of a chicken coop. We *gathered eggs for sale and killed the chickens to eat. And, yes, that was part of my duties – to gather the eggs **and** to kill and dress-out the chickens.*

It never failed – every Easter brought with it the season for baby chicks. We always had a passel of chicks we dyed and sold. They were the cutest little things. I recall parents would come to our farm the Saturday before Easter and pick out a pink, blue, green or yellow chick – sometimes one of every color – and take them away. I hated to see them go, having become attached to every one of them. They were my babies, my hatchlings. The mother hen would be some kind of upset that her baby chicks were being taken from her. My heart always ached for her loss.

~ ~ ~

Easter Unfolds

While I began to understand its flavor early in my childhood, the humbling significance of the Easter celebration would not unfold for me until around the age of eleven. I felt blessed to rise early on Easter for the Sunrise Service. The more I began to understand the security of God's Word, the more I looked forward to any opportunity for exposure to the message. My heart was full of expectancy as we rushed out to the field to await sunrise along with the others who had gathered. I was up at sunrise almost every day on the farm, but busy about my chores. If I had a moment to daydream, I would stand and be spellbound in its majesty as it rose over the tall Southern pines. Those times did not present themselves frequently enough. But, it was an undisturbed viewing on those special Easter Sunrise days.

Stricken with awe, I would stand and capture the moment of the glorious daybreak. It felt as if no one else stood beside me. The earth was still. The sound of chirping birds waking to the new dawn was melodic. The air was crisp and fresh; the hues more vibrant than I was certain I'd ever witnessed. A few farmhouses in the distance looked like postage stamps with glimmers of light like stars sprinkled among them.

I focused on the sky. God had His eyes only on me as I watched day break into unexpected beauty. The very essence of God swung open the door to Paradise and welcomed His children for a glimpse of Heaven's finest. Each Easter season, the spirit that swept across Earth was one of rapture, and as the day unfolded, it was more magnificent than my heart could stand. I felt a keen sense of love, yet I was barely aware of what that should feel like at all.

I was always hopeful on Easter – hopeful that Whoever it was we came to celebrate would find me acceptable and as special as I felt that one day out of each year. I was a child starved to feel accepted, starved to feel special, and starved to know Love. And growing in the knowledge of His promises, I had come to feel comfortable dreaming of and yearning for such things.

Ah, Easter! What a grand day it was. It was a fond memory of my childhood. After the day was spent, it was back to the farm and life as I knew it. Days would again become desolate for me. They would be tumultuous, anger-ridden, and fearful. The home would again be filled with abuse, mistrust, and void of love.

~~~

Homecoming Sunday never presented itself with the same flavor as Easter. While it was special because it was a time away from the farm, it was just a long day at church winding up with a lot of good country cooking. "So, what made Easter different?" I often pondered. Perhaps it was the undisturbed Sunrise. Or, maybe it was the hope of Love for me that accompanied that time. Whatever it was, it was special. I was happy for the experience. The feeling of ownership was infusing me.

But, wait, could I own God? Was He someone who would be mine? Was this Jesus that died on the cross and rose from the grave, the same one we celebrated at Easter, did He really die because He loved me, too? Was I that special to him? Could this be? If He loved me that much, then He was mine. And that meant I was His. So, yes, I could "own" God. I could claim Jesus as my Lord. He was mine. All mine. He was my Sunrise Love.

I would not fully appreciate Easter's significance until I was baptized at the age of twelve. It was then I would learn the meaning behind "raised to walk in the newness of life." I had read about that in my Gideons' Bible. I had read the verse from Romans about baptism countless times. But, until I stood my ground about going to church, this young mind couldn't grasp the full knowledge of the Word. Once I became enlightened about the obedience, I was eager to accept the Lord Jesus as my Savior and to be baptized.

~~~

> That's what baptism into the life of Jesus means. When we are lowered into the water, it is like the burial of Jesus; when we are raised up out of the water, it is like the resurrection of Jesus. Each of us is raised into a light-filled world by our Father so that we can see where we're going in our new grace-sovereign country.
> ~Romans 6:3-5 (The Message Bible)

~~~

Forgiveness ... Without that element, there can be no release, and certainly no pardon.

11

Part 1: Prisoner to the Past

Onward, Christian Soldiers

Getting to the water would be the challenge and my next step in this hallmark memory. Farmers help each other out. We had some friends who lived about two miles down the way on our rural route. Not social acquaintances. We only helped one another by sharing family members for tobacco responsibilities. I don't know that the adult Harveys ever set foot in our home, nor our parents in their home. The kids did bop in and out occasionally. My brothers were good friends with the boys; they were crazy about me and frequently found reason to come around. I would have enjoyed camaraderie with the girl. We were friends in passing. No real sharing. We rode the same bus and exchanged casual chitchat.

Vicky was a sweet girl and might have made a great bonding link. I was too afraid to allow anyone close to me for fear she would want to do those kind of girlie things, like come home and spend the night with me. Heavens! Fear and dread swept over me at that very thought. It would have been horrible. Could have been disastrous. I wanted to protect them and not expose them to anything that might bring them harm, or me embarrassment.

Neighbors needed help with their tobacco crop. I was always eager to make money, in light of the fact I got no stipend for chores around the house, save for the fifty cents to get in the movies and to buy popcorn and a soda. (*Yeah, you got a lot for your quarter in those days!*) While working beside them in their fields, I learned they went to church. Eagerness enveloped my face, and they suggested I catch a ride with them. I readily accepted the offer. We agreed on a time for pickup.

Hitching a Ride

It took some doing, but I persuaded Dad to allow me to go to church with the Harveys. That first Sunday worked very well. No hitches. I stood patiently at the roadside with my Gideons' Bible in hand and waited for my ride. I can recall tipping up on my toes, looking feverishly down that *flat* road to see if I could catch a glimpse of the top of their car. Anxious for the real opportunity to listen to someone talk about the things I'd been reading in my Bible, to hear the stories come to life, and satisfy a hunger for the knowledge of Jesus invigorated my soul that morning. I felt like I was going to a ball, a place where my heart could dance and sing.

The sun was warm against my face, my little heart was pounding to a different beat, and I was like a bird let out of its cage. I was not standing on this roadside hitching a ride to school. I was going to church! A new adventure. A safe adventure. It was a place where people would love you, accept you, and befriend you without reservation. Hurrah! *Right.* It was a place I wanted to visit, to check out for myself, and today, I was on my way.

"Sorry, we're running a little late this morning, Joyce. Were you standing here a long time?" Mr. Harvey asked.

"Oh, it's okay. Not long at all," I replied. I wasn't about to make him feel bad. He was obliging me.

"We may be a little bit late for church, but we won't miss much," he added. And, off we went on our Sunday morning journey.

It was a good twenty-minute ride to the church. There was small chitchat exchanged between the family members. I was quiet. I'd never been off with anyone outside of work affairs before. This was all new, and a bit uncertain. I didn't know how other families talked to each other. I was a bit uneasy about the unknown. But, they were nice people, and they were taking me to church. It couldn't be all that bad.

Instant Friends

I recall pulling up to that sacred ground of Pleasant Way Baptist Church. My face was plastered against the window of the Harveys' old Buick. The church was the most beautiful sight I'd ever seen. I emerged from the car, stepping into the white sandy lot. The majestic oaks clustered around, with great beards of Spanish moss suspended from their sprawling branches. It was a white wood-framed building; nothing fancy, but, oh, so welcoming. My heart was pounding out of my chest. My petite legs rubbery with anticipation, I began ascending the steps leading up to its open door. A gentle breeze brushed against my back, encouraging me to step inside for a dose of deliberate understanding.

A gentleman, Brother Gene, stood at the door with a Texas-size grin on his face, welcoming the Harveys and their new little friend. The pianist raised the roof as she cranked up the congregation with a lively, peppy arrangement of "When We All

Get to Heaven." Voices were clamoring in praise. The older, squawky grandmoms and creaky bass gramps chimed in a beat out of step with the more fluid monotones. Paired with the melodious, God-gifted talents, it was a joyful noise unto the Lord resounding across that plot of holy ground.

"Who is this beautiful gal you brought with you this morning, Brother?"

"This is Joyce. She decided to tag along for the ride today."

"We're glad you came, Joyce. You're going to love it here," said Brother Gene, offering me his right hand of fellowship. We were instant friends.

Church took to me immediately. We were soulmates. It was the friend I had so wanted to share my life with. It was the companion I had waited for forever. Church would be the refuge home should have been. It would be the one outlet I grew to anticipate each week. This house of worship would become a soft place, perhaps the gentlest caress I would ever come to know. This new institution in my life would develop within me a hope for a brighter day. Church was my link to the lifeline that would grant me a pardon from the sin that had made me a prisoner. It wasn't my sin that held me captive, but the sins of others. But, it was enslaving nonetheless. I would soon discover the source of freedom. I had been introduced to a means of stepping out of bondage through a comforting, promising plan called salvation. I had been handed the key that would unlock my heart. *Now, to get out of prison.*

Being unfamiliar with the songs didn't matter to me. I grabbed a hymnbook and joined right in. I did have an ear for music. It just wasn't as attuned as it could have been had my granddaddy been able to live out a dream in me. I laid low on the verses, but hitchhiked on the choruses and sang to the top of my lungs. I was introduced to "Onward, Christian Soldiers" that day. I repressed the urge to march to the beat. I got lost in the lyrics and shouted out the refrain. *That was easy, and they sang every verse – all five.* Little did I know it would be a charge for battle in my life.

~~~

Onward, Christian soldiers, marching as to war,

with the cross of Jesus going on before.

Christ, the royal Master, leads against the foe;

forward into battle see his banners go!

Onward, Christian soldiers, marching as to war,

with the cross of Jesus going on before.

At the sign of triumph Satan's host doth flee;

on then, Christian soldiers, on to victory!

Hell's foundations quiver at the shout of praise;

brothers, lift your voices, loud your anthems raise.

Onward, Christian soldiers, marching as to war,

with the cross of Jesus going on before.

~Lyrics: Sabine Baring-Gould

~ ~ ~

Engaged in a Hug

I scoped the crowd, taking in all the nuances of this new adventure. Imagine my surprise when I spotted the backs of the heads of my grandparents! There he was – Granddaddy! And Nannie! Oh, my goodness. They were here in church with me!

It had been several years since I had seen either one of them. I scarce could concentrate on the service. Brother Hobbs would do a masterful job at preaching, as he always did, but my heart was engaged in a hug. I wanted to run to my grandparents right then, and I wanted the preacher to get done so I could do just that.

What was I saying? Here was my opportunity to listen to some of the stories I had been reading about, and I was missing it. I was tuning him out. My mind was racing with memories of the good times in my grandparents' home. I was wondering why I had forgotten this was their home church. Why had I not made the connection? But then, I was very young when we had been forced apart. But now, here I was in the same room with my granddaddy once again. My gaze was fixed upon him. He was small up against Nannie's big frame. Sitting low in his seat, his whole countenance revealed his humble, gentle, and kind spirit. I was certain they didn't see me come in; else they would have come to greet me.

I was suddenly antsy for the service to end. Or, was I really ready for that? Would I miss the whole reason I came? I thanked God for answering a prayer I had been praying – to be reunited with my grandparents. I believed it was Him who had orchestrated this moment in time. But now, I had come to hear a message about God and Jesus, and how He loves me. My ears perked up, and I focused on Brother Hobbs' sermon.

Insistence with a Promise

He was a pleasant personality, this man of the cloth. Warmth exuded from his demeanor. It wasn't like the hellfire and brimstone I was familiar with at the Primitive Baptist gatherings. He would talk about the blessing of this forgiving Jesus, His saving power of the cross, and how easy it was to come to know Him and let our troubles rest on Him. Brother Hobbs' smile was big and kind. His pleading was not condemning. He would offer everyone the redeeming grace of God, but his insistence was one with promise.

~~~

I sat there at altar call, feeling this was probably something I should do – go up and be saved. But, the chains restricted me. I still felt shackled to a life that had limitations, boundaries, borders that I couldn't cross, and walls I dare not scale. I sat in the pew, frozen with fear. I was paralyzed with dread of what could be, what most likely would be if I stepped out in faith without first reporting to "the guard." I would wait. I would have to manage this decision carefully. This was one day, one moment in time. What would the next day bring? It was all too uncertain in our household. I had caught Dad in a good mood. What would it be like by the time I got home? It was a toss of the coin.

~~~

The Reunion

It was a grand reunion after church. Brief, but grand. I wanted to linger but couldn't detain the Harveys. Granddaddy's heart was lighter, as was mine. But, we both walked away with an unspoken sadness not knowing if this time would come again. I resolved it would. Come hell or high water, I would be back. It would take some doing, but I would return. I now had hope, something I had not considered prior to today.

~~~

> May the LORD answer you when you are in distress;
> may the name of the God of Jacob protect you.
>
> May he send you help from the sanctuary
> and grant you support from Zion.
>
> May he remember all your sacrifices
> and accept your burnt offerings.
>
> May he give you the desire of your heart
> and make all your plans succeed.
>
> May we shout for joy over your victory
> and lift up our banners in the name of our God.
>
> May the LORD grant all your requests.
>
> Now this I know:
> The LORD gives victory to his anointed.

> He answers him from his heavenly sanctuary
> with the victorious power of his right hand.
>
> Some trust in chariots and some in horses,
> but we trust in the name of the LORD our God.
>
> They are brought to their knees and fall,
>
> but we rise up and stand firm.
>
> LORD, give victory to the king!
> Answer us when we call!
>
> ~Psalm 20 (NIV)

~~~

A New Hope

The desire to return to Pleasant Way Baptist was planted. Not only to see my grandparents, but also to feed off the nourishment I had experienced in that one precious hour. I was onto something ... something big. Something different. Something refreshing. Something pure -- the purest form of love I had ever known. My heart was suddenly alive and caught a new excitement about my destiny. Could I become a new creature in Christ? Could I get out of what seemed a perilous plight? Could this be part of the assurance God had given me at the mantel that day? Yes, I had hope. It was fresh. It was inviting. It was mine!

12

Part 1: Prisoner to the Past

The Battle

My newfound addiction to church soon met with much resistance. Dad and I had managed to develop a ritual. On Saturday I'd ask permission to go to church the next day. Dad agreed that if I got all my chores done, I could go. Each week, he added a few more things to an already-lengthy list of tasks to perform. I managed, however, to get every job completed and would begin to get ready to catch my ride. The unfortunate thing is that Sunday mornings came after Saturday nights. He'd be at a honky-tonk, drunk and with his lady friend(s), come home in the wee morning hours, and he and mother would begin arguing. One thing would lead to another and…. Well, you get the picture.

Regardless of our previous day's agreement, my church day typically met with confrontation. Much to my chagrin, I did get my temper from my father. The stubborn, determined traits I inherited from Mother. Those traits coupled with my newly acquired belief that "I can do everything through Him who gives me strength" (Phil. 4:13, NIV) made for a real match of wits. It usually ended with Dad taking his belt to me, and he assumed that would end the argument. His artillery was no match for my headstrong determination. The battle was on. I stood my ground, armored up with temper, stubbornness and God, and waited at the roadside bearing stripes up and down my back and legs as proof of my resolve.

Little did I realize that a hefty portion of his resistance for my going to church was his knowledge of Mother's parents' attendance at Pleasant Way. I had been careful not to say anything to Dad about seeing them there. I knew the outcome would not be favorable had he had an inkling of an idea they were attending. *I still marvel at God's paving the way for me and giving me the strength to stand strong in fierce battle.*

Hungry for God's grace, I found my way to church almost every Sunday. If the Harveys were headed there, I was along for the ride. I clung to the instructions of Brother Hobbs. It wouldn't be long before I convinced my dad to "allow" Mother and the others to come along, too. *He would join later.* We were a family starved for God's love. *I was surprised Mother would actually come. He didn't always mean to "allow" her to do something. If she didn't read him just right, she would have to answer for it later.* Mother was a barren soul, having been stripped of dignity and self-value. This was nothing new to her; just misplaced by life. The timing was ideal.

~~~

God's timing is always perfect. I have come to know He's the right-on-time Lord of my life. Being patient and waiting on His answer to a prayer is the most difficult part of the process. But it's crucial. It's critical for the success of anything we do. God cannot be rushed, you see. He's all-knowing. He's got the big screen right there, and we're not privy to the final act. It's the wait that's often boring, or downright unnerving.

When you're in a difficult situation, one that is particularly painful – whether physical or emotional, impatience is bound to set in. That's when you dig in your heels and get resolved to allow Him to work through you. It will do little more than frustrate you to do anything less than wait.

I'm not suggesting to anyone who is in a physically, sexually, or emotionally abusive situation to wait and let God tie down your assailant. Let's be real here. What I am suggesting is that you break free of your pain. Trust God to take care of you. Stand strong against your foe. If it is someone who overpowers you, find a way to get out. God does not desire for any one of His children to be harmed. He loves you too much. It's a deliberate union of heart, mind and soul to know and follow God's will at all costs. Each situation must be looked at, because there are varying degrees of not only infliction of pain, but also the degree to which people tolerate it.

Abuse is a difficult situation to go through, to handle, to get free of. Many abused women have choices. Most children do not. Once out of the situation, no one has to hang onto its ugly past. When you allow past injustices to haunt you, you thwart God's ultimate will and purpose in your life. Oh, my, what blessings await when you step out of that prison of the past!

God's timing. It's perfect. It's our resistance to His call in our lives that hangs up the ol' hands on the clock. We get stuck at a bewitching hour because we think God forgot to show up. He's never late! It is our impatience that prohibits God from recharging our batteries and starting the timepiece in our lives all over again. Instead, we stay lost in time with our pain, and the memory of the perpetrator haunting us. Chained-up memories, shackled-down hope. Staying locked in the prison of the past detains us from experiencing God's magnificent care and provision, and the abundant joy He has waiting for us in the free world!

~~~

A Cleansing Rebirth

It wouldn't be long before Mother and clan *(minus Dad for now)* would become regulars at Pleasant Way. Mother loaded up that car every Sunday with all the young 'uns and we struck out for church. The relationship with my mom's parents was strained at first, but soon rekindled. I was the first to walk the aisle. I could stand it no longer. Propelled from my seat by a force too mighty to resist, I made my way to Brother Hobbs. Tears of joy streaming down my face, a smile that couldn't be contained, I became a Child of the King.

Mother and the boys would follow suite shortly thereafter. We would be scheduled to make provisions for our baptism into Christ. It was to be a glorious day. My long-time prayer was going to be answered in God's way, in His timing. He had worked it out.

The cold Alapaha River in South Georgia would render me slave to serve a Risen Savior. I, too, had been resurrected – my old life now dead, my new life just beginning! I had been saved through the slain blood of this Jesus. I had a cleansing rebirth. Never again would I stand at a sunrise and wonder if I was special. I now knew how special I was. Easter would be more prominent in my life than ever before. The Triumphant Entry, the Last Supper, the Betrayal, the Garden of Gethsemane, the Trial, the Crucifixion, and the Resurrection would merge into a passion for *me* that would shape every day, not just Easter, into a world of acceptance, hope, and, yes, even and especially love. This Savior was no longer a story in some book that I read by flashlight underneath my covers in bed. He was now my new personal friend. Jesus had become my biggest hope of redemption. I was searching for a touch of His wisdom. It would take time, but I had nothing else better to do than wait on God … and grow up.

13

Part 1: Prisoner to the Past

Change in the Making

My baptism set a new course for my life. It also introduced me to a fresh new understanding of life. The impact it would have on me was transforming and would serve eventually to bring me to serving the Lord alongside a minister husband. But, that would be some seven years later.

There was still the problem with the warden of our home prison. Outside of prayer and persistence about going to church, I don't know what would have moved my father to load up with us to go to church that first Sunday. We were all surprised, and a bit nervous. What if he acted out when he saw Granddaddy and

Nannie? Would there be a scene? I didn't know if he had been told, or if he always knew. But something was changing. A slow transformation was taking hold in our home.

What were we doing differently than before? Praying. Bringing the preacher home for dinner on Sundays. *That was really different!* My dad was warming up to Brother Hobbs. The preacher was a common, ordinary man. He drove down from Tifton, Georgia to preach each Sunday; and our place was on his route home. It worked out perfectly. Mother and I would put out a spread. We were great cooks. She had taught me the art when I was big enough to stand on a five-gallon lard bucket. She would turn it upside down, I'd climb right up, and she'd give me step-by-step instructions on making homemade biscuits. By the time I was nine, I could whip up mean pans of biscuits, yeast rolls, and banana pudding made from scratch. Each was delicious. *My biscuits were never as yummy as Mother's. She had the touch for rolling out the biscuits in the palms of her hands. But as for yeast rolls, she wasn't even in the race with me. They became my specialty items. As for the pudding, you couldn't tell ours apart (still a favorite around my home). And I have the original pan that thousands of makings have been served in.*

It was only a matter of weeks after Brother Hobbs broke bread with my family that we would see a change in the making. Each Sunday at church, the message would be compelling, absolutely convicting for even the worst of sinners. Dad was right there amongst them. The old hymn, "The vilest offender who truly believes, that moment from Jesus a pardon receives" must have been written with him in mind. Dad was standing beside me shuffling his feet again as we bellowed out that old mantra. He squirmed all throughout the sermon that day. I didn't ignore his restlessness; I capitalized on it. I began praying during the sermon. I prayed, *Lord, may today be the day that he claims you as Lord of his life. Let him turn his life around, God. Please save my Daddy.*

There was no thought in my head that it would have to be my father's will that must concede to the calling of his heart. God was ready for him to make the commitment; had been all along. God would rather my dad give up his riotous way of life – his addiction to the bottle, to women, to being enslaved to his anger and bitterness. God's will for his life was in concert with mine. But neither of us could make that decision for him. It would have to be a radical change in his heart – a change that would touch his life in a way that he would walk away from the stranglehold sin had on him.

The invitational song began. I kept praying. Junior kept shuffling his feet, fidgeting with his hymnbook, mouthing the words. Abruptly I was pushed aside. Could it be? Could he be making his way toward the preacher? It was true! His heart had caved. His will had broken. My father was surrendering his life to Christ. I glanced at my mother's face of disbelief, but nothing could defy the relief in her eyes. My granddad cracked a grin and shook his head. Nannie's stern-set jaw never changed.

To God Be the Glory

I beamed as Dad made his Good Confession, and Brother Hobbs welcomed him to the family of God. There was a change in the making. My heart was fuller than I could ever imagine it to be. I walked out of church that day with hope in my heart, peace on my mind, and laughter on my lips. It was a strange personality awakening in me. I was light-hearted. The weight of the world was off my shoulders. It was a new day. I couldn't get the song out of my head, for He was worthy of praise!

~~~

> To God be the glory, great things He hath done,
> So loved He the world that He gave us His Son,
> Who yielded His life our redemption to win,
> And opened the life-gate that all may go in.
>
> Praise the Lord, praise the Lord,
> Let the earth hear His voice;
> Praise the Lord, praise the Lord,
> Let the people rejoice;
> Oh, come to the Father, through Jesus the Son,
> And give Him the glory; great things He hath done.

> Oh, perfect redemption, the purchase of blood,
> To every believer the promise of God;
> The vilest offender who truly believes,
> That moment from Jesus a pardon receives.
>
> ~Lyrics by: Fanny J. Crosby

~~~

14

Part 1: Prisoner to the Past

The More Things Change

Our family found ourselves on the Valdosta side of the world as much as we were in Lakeland. Dad got very involved in church. He brought his honky-tonking cronies with him. Some of them caught the fever; others didn't. It wasn't long before he was playing his guitar and singing with an ensemble: three men and a lady. Their performance, naturally, would require numerous practices.

It had been a nice respite from the chaos that our household once knew. But, we barely got to breathe in the peace before all hell broke loose, because Satan returned with a vengeance. Things began to rumble again in Mother and Dad's bedroom. With the new addition on our house, my bedroom door was just across from theirs. Walls were thin – too thin. You could hear everything. It had made for very sleepless nights. The rumblings were unsettling. I knew there was trouble brewing; I just didn't know how long before the lid would blow.

I had my suspicions about what was going on even before the storm was brewing at home. I was hoping against hope it wasn't true. But, Brother Hobbs always said you really had to be careful once you gave your soul to Jesus, because Satan would be after it "right quick." He wasted no time tracking down my dad again.

New Spark of Interest

The starry-eyed look in Dad's eyes was more than singing for Jesus in front of a congregation of fifty-plus. Mother hadn't mistaken his demeanor. It was a familiar trait he had exhibited in the past. She was reverting to her old habits of despondency. Slumping back into a depression. Her anger and frustration were returning. She was impatient and sharp with her tongue. Things were slipping back to the way they had been.

The next time I would feel the wrath of anger at her hands, which I was no stranger to, would be when she discovered my diary. I was foolish enough to have written my notion about my dad's involvement with Angie, the *lady* in their ensemble. I had been wise to his shenanigans for a long time, too. Wise beyond my years regarding flirtations between men and women, it didn't take long for me to be concerned and begin praying for intervention in this new spark of interest.

Mother confronted me out under the Mimosa tree with my journal in hand. I was confused as to why she would attack me about something I had written. I wasn't the one who was betraying her. It was by far the worst beating she had ever inflicted on me. My heart was broken more so than the infractions on my skin. *Years later I would come to understand I was the only one she could take out her frustrations on. She was no match for my dad. So, I would bear the brunt of her broken heart. Still no excuse, but an understanding helps somewhat.*

The Kiss of Near Death

Angie and her husband had three boys. The two older were definite "boyfriend" material. I was coming of age to be interested in the opposite sex. Even the good senses can't defy nature when everything in your life is normal except home. Billy was a year younger than me, Tony a year older. My eyes were fixed on Tony, but Billy's eyes were on me.

We had visited their home for our parents to practice for Sunday's service. By this time, Dad was under Mother's watchful eye, and that left the kids to be on their own. I always seemed to have one, or two, attached at the hip. The older boys coaxed me outside. Their plot was to have me kiss Billy. Or, so they thought. Billy was not in favor of it any more than I was, so that wasn't going to happen. The boys grabbed us both, pressed our lips together, and Billy and I had kissed!

Who would have thought it would have created such trauma in Billy's life? He ran into the house like his arm had been cut off, screaming and raising a raucous. My brothers and I looked at each other knowing *this can't be good.* We were right. Billy's mother was fit to be tied. My dad was consoling her. Mother was fuming from frustration with what she had been witnessing inside, and now that we had caused such a big fuss, and it involved me kissing a boy, she was beside herself. What a mess!

I was yanked by the arm and demanded to get in the car. Dad's only words were that he would take care of me when we got home. The twenty-five-minute distance that separated the two houses felt like an eternity, yet seemed to end very abruptly. There would be no recompense. My brothers would offer no fault of their own for fear it would make matters worse. They were well aware of how volatile Dad was capable of becoming. We had not seen this side of him for a few months, so any pent-up, leftover anger would soon erupt.

He had barely parked the car when I was snatched by the hair of the head and dragged inside the house, kicking me to my bedroom. I crouched in a fetal position as he continued to kick me while taking the belt out of his pants. The belt buckle kept striking my hands and arms as I covered my head. In his uncontrolled anger, he grabbed me and began stripping my clothes from my body. I was thrown facedown on the bed, hands and feet tied to the posts, and was beaten until I fell into an unconscious state. But, he had made restitution for Angie's "little boy," and in his state of adultery, that was important to him.

~~~

My face was unscathed. Clothes cover multitudes of sins. My hands were visibly abused. Maneuvering was a real challenge. Breathing was difficult. I was in obvious distress emotionally. Yet, no teacher showed an ounce of concern. There was no advocate for a child experiencing abuse. There were others in the school. I recognized it. Why didn't they?

I'm grateful for the awareness we have in place in the school systems today. Yet, I am also aware that not everyone gets the attention he or she deserves. I'm also aware that perpetrators get off in our justice system time and time again. Whether physical and/or sexual abuse, the crime is not brought to justice because of technicalities, or because kids are embarrassed or simply won't testify against their offender for fear of what will happen if the offenders don't get sent to prison. So, the kids go back in the home, only to be abused again. The cycle continues, and it is passed down through generational sin.

God will deal with people who harm His children. He tells us in Matthew 18:6: "If anyone causes one of these little ones—those who believe in me—to stumble, it would be better for them to have a large millstone hung around their neck and to be drowned in the depths of the sea."

~~~

Business as Usual

The affair would last for another year. Mother reverted to her depression and despondency, all the while expected to carry out her laborious lifestyle. Dad gravitated from bad to worse. So did home life. The news broke. The attempt to hide it from the kids fell short. Angie and her family would move away suddenly. Life would resume to pre-saved days in our household. Anger was out of control. There was no more laughter. No warmth. Only bedlam.

My oldest brother would go off to battle in Viet Nam. Mother experienced even more stress and became more dependent on drugs and alcohol. Dad was back in the juke joints, cavorting with women, drinking heavily, and reverting to his abusive mannerisms. He would make life miserable for all.

Waiting on God's deliverance this time was the hardest part. It would call for self-control and even anger management on my part. It would call for forgiveness in larger doses than most teenagers are capable of producing on a day-in/day-out basis without considerable rebellion. Abuse would continue to plague our home. It would continue to attempt to destroy my heart for God and my witness to His promises. I had no other recourse but to trust the Lord. I would lean on him and wait. Jesus loved me, this I knew. I was sustained and, therefore, maintained my steady path.

~~~

What is the source of your strength? Who sustains you when all else seems lost? When your world goes nowhere but spiraling down, who will grab your hand and pull you out of the vortex of despair? The Lord will deliver you from your confusion and anxiety. My circumstances were less than favorable, and He was there for me.

Some would say I gained false hope at Dad's short walk with Christ. It wasn't false hope at all. I caught a glimpse of what life lived with Christ in the mix would be. I rejoiced in that window of time. Yes, I would have preferred the "enchanted" life to continue. All of us wanted that. And to this day, I believe even Dad would have preferred it. His flesh overcame his good sense.

The time with Christ in the midst of our home was peace wrapped up in love. Forgiveness had been instituted. Healing was taking place. Once wounds were incised again, scars were deeper, wider, and more unsightly. Balancing insecurity and distrust with anger, resentment and bitterness is a no-win scenario. With those ingredients being all that the adults factored into their days, it left nothing but pandemonium for our nights.

The fact that bears greater weight at this point is that God did not alter one iota the drama being played out in our home. It was man's free will, once again, that would step off the path of faith, just as he stepped onto it. God would have continued His faithfulness to my dad, like He did me. I counted on His help because I had been witness to that authenticity. Once we place our faith in the Word of God, we accept that truth as absolute. Regardless of how we may fall away from those solid teachings, God says what He means and means what He says.

That knowledge alone is a great source of strength. It's always man who steps away from God's will for his life. I would learn that praising Him, even in the midst of trials, would be a significant aspect of my faith. So, praise Him, I did. Depend upon Him, I could. Worship Him, I would.

~~~

> We have this hope as an anchor for the soul, firm and secure.
>
> ~Hebrews 6:19 (NIV)

~~~

15

Part 1: Prisoner to the Past

Deliverance

Pray for a Webby? What's that? Those familiar with my ministry have heard my testimony of how I began praying when I was twelve for my husband. My prayer was simple: "God, please send someone to teach me how to love." He sent the most wonderful godly husband. Had I looked the world over, I would have never handpicked a man with a sweeter heart. I am grateful I integrated God into my decision for a soulmate.

Choosing a mate is a huge decision in a person's life. Choosing someone you will spend the rest of your life with should never be taken lightly. I knew very little about the world.

As exposed as I had been to the *naked* truth (no pun intended) about how despicable men could be, I would have been totally inept at making the choice for a spouse in my life.

I knew nothing about love. Yes, the spiritual love was growing in me. The connection with Christ was strong in my life. I was not a crystal pure young girl nor teenager. I would fall short and disappoint God at many levels. *I would not want anyone to be misguided in thinking I lived a pristine life. I was far from perfect. No one is. But, I deferred to God more than not. That's a plus for a young person, and especially one whose home lacked honor for Him. Not perfect, but preparing.* There would be seasons I would place God on hold. Wherever I was in my walk, I stayed put. There were days when I would take two steps backward. I didn't enjoy regression, but it happened. I would find myself having to re-plow ground once turned. I was no different from any other Christian. Life was hard: harder for me than most, but not as difficult as some people had it. *I never take for granted that my life was more difficult than others'. When you think you have it bad, look around you – someone always has it worse, regardless of the circumstances.*

I wouldn't lay down that prayer for love. Even though I would be devoted to a relationship with a great young man, I continued the prayer. I didn't know what the face of love would look like, but my heart was not settled with what I had seen. There must be more to love than feelings. I wanted to go deeper than the mere surface. I wanted to know the full breadth of affection, the complete width of devotion, and the total depth of commitment. I would not learn that in an environment where Christ was absent. I desired to set my sights on someone whose heart was united with God's. I believed with every fiber within me God would reveal that to me in time. I had already sampled His timetable phenomenon. (*Remember, He kept my "friend" at bay until I was 17.*) This request was not unreasonable. I would wait. I was familiar with His hand of assurance. When He had answered that prayer, my heart would know. I was certain of that.

~~~

> The secret things belong to the LORD our God, but the things revealed belong to us and to our children forever, that we may follow all the words of this law.
>
> ~Deuteronomy 29:29

~~~

The process of blocking out bad memories is not always a solo exercise.

16

Part 1: Prisoner to the Past

Significant Revelation

People often ask: "If you could change any part of your childhood, what would it be?" I don't have to think about that response. If I thought for an instant I would be less likely to have the personal relationship I share with Christ, I'd go through every day again – all the abuse, every tear I shed, every sleepless night – exactly the same!

The more I learned about the grueling death of our Savior, the easier it was to endure the battles with my father on Sunday mornings. As unforgiving as his belt was striking my bare back and legs, my stripes were nothing compared to what our Savior suffered. Isaiah 53 tells us "by those very stripes we are healed." It became an honor for this 12-year-old girl to stand on the roadside with a wounded spirit and stripes bearing witness of my devotion to God.

The hope I anticipated each Easter Sunrise as a little girl was now very much a part of my life – still a little girl, but now a child of the King! Imagine how powerful that comfort was to a child who felt trapped in a life out of control.

Jesus introduced me to love – something foreign to me. He compensated for the longing in my heart. It had been a constant ache until He moved in. Throughout my childhood, I would strive for acceptance from my mother in many ways. I knew she loved me. She loved all her children. She just didn't really have time to show love. There were only so many hours in a day. Hers were spent before the day even dawned. Her sacrifice was amazing in hindsight. Her motherly instinct for protection and provision for her children was in large part what kept her in the home to endure the horrendous abuse. That should've been enough to satisfy my heart. But, it wasn't. I continued to need her approval, her tenderness, and her love.

~~~

Every child is born with a desire to love, to bond at birth. I have wept with many people who have been through an adoption process. A child who was adopted by a loving family sometimes confuses the adoptive parents. The parents invested time, energy, finances, and everything that accompanies a parent-child relationship. They truly felt like the real *parents. However, the child, now an adult, loves them deeply, yet still feels as though something is missing. The child will not rest until he or she finds the biological mother and/ or father.*

What ingredient is missing that hasn't been supplied by the family who reared them? No one could deny the bond that occurs from womb to mother's arms. Mother's scent, her pulse, temperature, sound, even her touch has been a constant for nine months. Ejected from the familiar, the baby desires to return to the familiar. It is what affords the child immediate comfort. It is instinctive. It's how God designed it. It was never His intent to have them ripped from their mother's womb for premature disposal as though they were devoid of feeling. Nor did God intend for a child to be separated at birth because of the inconvenient timing of his/her advent. At conception a child becomes acquainted with his/her forever guardian of life. Heartbeats are synchronized in rhythm — mom and child, in perfect harmony. The spirits reflect in unison a history shared only between the two.

And so it is, should separation ensue, a difficult conflict of the hearts begins. The child-rearing parents will fear they will lose a part of their history. On the part of the child, it will be an unceasing desire, and perhaps a life's mission, to penetrate the eyes of the birthing mother. It is there they will find the answer to the question that haunts them most: Did you really love me?

~ ~ ~

Motherhood Revelations

Once I became a mother, I thought I would understand more why Mother would not step in to protect me against the sexual abuse that plagued me throughout my homelife. Why would she be silent on that lone ride home from the doctor's office that day? Why would she never revisit the subject? Why wouldn't she defend me? No answer came to those questions after motherhood. In fact, it became an even more confusing issue in my heart.

I did, however, gain a better understanding of how little time she had to give to any of her children. With the demands of work, not only in the home but also in the fields, the physical toll to her health, and the emotional drain with all the turmoil, where would she fit in special, quality time and attention for eight children? It was too much for one individual to achieve. Honestly, I don't know how she did everything day in and day out. God rest her soul. She is enjoying living beyond our imagination. Praise God!

Forgiveness in Daily Doses

It is forgiveness that would have me reestablish a relationship with my mom. Had I not chosen to forgive, there would be little reason to attempt to step out of the prison of home, whether my knight in shining armor arrived or not. Forgiveness was a daily routine for me. I was always having to forgive some infraction. I'm convinced it was what kept me together emotionally, allowed me to function physically, and paved the way for a healthier life after home.

The formula was in the Word. Forgiveness would be the secret to stepping outside of the prison, both while I lived there and once I left home. Without that element, there could be no release, and certainly no pardon. It would be a significant revelation in my life to begin to grasp the power of forgiveness. It would be dispensed in daily doses. I had not yet fully experienced it, but I would in my maturation process.

~~~

His divine power has given us everything we need for a godly life through our knowledge of him who called us by his own glory and goodness. Through these he has given us his very great and precious promises, so that through them you may participate in the divine nature, having escaped the corruption in the world caused by evil desires.

For this very reason, make every effort to add to your faith goodness; and to goodness, knowledge; and to knowledge, self-control; and to self-control, perseverance; and to perseverance, godliness; and to godliness, mutual affection; and to mutual affection, love. For if you possess these qualities in increasing measure, they will keep you from being ineffective and unproductive in your knowledge of our Lord Jesus Christ. But whoever does not have them is nearsighted and blind, forgetting that they have been cleansed from their past sins.

Therefore, my brothers and sisters, make every effort to confirm your calling and election. For if you do these things, you will never stumble, and you will receive a rich welcome into the eternal kingdom of our Lord and Savior Jesus Christ.

~2 Peter 1:3-11 (NIV)

Stitched Together

From mantel prayer to the love prayer, God granted my petitions. The prayer of this 12-year-old girl's heart, "Lord, please send someone to teach me how to love" was as good as done. Little did I know God had already begun to prepare my husband's heart to fill my request. He knew long before I asked that my heart would need restoration. Three years prior to that prayer rolling off my tongue, through the hands of a skilled surgeon, God repaired the hole in my husband's heart that, without being mended, would have claimed his life before he turned twenty-one. The stitch that darned his heart would make its way to mine, and our hearts would become one with God seven years later.

~~~

Jesus was the mysterious "whoever" I celebrated as a young girl awaiting sunrise. He was the hopeful expectation I returned for each year. He was the giver of life to one who felt uninhabited with feelings of worth. Jesus was the one who accepted me just as I was. God knew eons before I was conceived in my mother's womb that I would be in need of a complete restoration in my life, so He sent me my Sunrise Love. For God so loved ... me ... that He gave His only begotten Son, that if I just believe in Him, I shall have everlasting life. It was a significant revelation. The beauty of Jesus? He's everyone's Sunrise Love.

~~~

Dear friends, let us love one another, for love comes from God.
Everyone who loves has been born of God and knows God.
Whoever does not love does not know God, because God is love.
This is how God showed his love among us: He sent his one and
only Son into the world that we might live through him.
This is love: not that we loved God, but that he loved us
and sent his Son as an atoning sacrifice for our sins.

~ I John 4:7-10 (NIV)

Part 1: The Past

Life Lesson Plan 1

Women and men confide in me regarding the shackles that keep them hostage to their past. They truly desire to be released, but all attempts fail. They believe their prayers fall on deaf ears, because they deserved whatever injustice happened in their lives. Self-worth is destroyed. Self-confidence is denied the rites of passage in order to override their daunting, debilitating history.

As we continue to discuss the drama behind the particular circumstances surrounding the demise of their will to really live, we begin to work through the source of their imprisonment. Even though they have told the story, repeatedly lived it, played it out in their thoughts and dreams hundreds to perhaps thousands of times, I allow them the opportunity to share each sordid detail they desire to spill forth.

Interjecting God's Word while conversing, it evokes answers to questions they have forbidden themselves to express for years. Once they dispense with the situations beyond their control, they begin to realize some things were not their fault. Beginning to understand how the desires of the flesh cause men to sin against God, themselves, and others shifts the burden to the Savior who is equipped to shoulder it. The fog that has clouded their thinking begins to dissipate, and they begin to see their path to freedom.

Here are some take-away tools for you to incorporate into your journey to imminent release. Let's get started today.

Evaluate

(Read Romans 8 – We are more than conquerors!)

- **Evaluate each situation** that you struggle with. Others may surface later on. As memories invade your thoughts, go through this same exercise of evaluation. Don't stay shackled to fear. Becoming immobile prevents you from moving on. You can't step out of prison once the door is open if you choose to remain in your cell.

- **Admit or deny your responsibility** in the circumstances surrounding the event(s). This exercise will provide you with the key to rid yourself of the guilt for situations beyond your control.

- **Accept the role, if any, you played in the situation.** Evaluate where and why you were in the position to use poor judgment. For example, immaturity may have played a huge part in your lack of wisdom at the time.

- **Pray and ask for forgiveness** immediately for your participation in causing situations in which you admit part or full responsibility. Mustard-seed faith must be implemented in order to obtain this key. Believing God can, will, and has already made adequate provisions for your forgiveness is crucial in order to unlock the chains around your heart.

- **Praise** the One who stood in your gap. Always praise Him!

- **Rejoice in His protection of you.** You have reason to celebrate being a survivor. You are one!

- **Repeat these steps as often as necessary.** Jesus has opened the door for you. Trust Him, take His hand, and walk with Him. You don't have to go it alone. Not only does Jesus know the way, but He *is* the way!

> *It's often the hardships and trials someone has suffered that bring the lessons in life.*

Part 2:

Fugitive in the Present

17

Part 2: Fugitive in the Present

Turning Point

My thumbnail sketch of life growing up is indicative of how many people become shackled to a past – staying locked in a prison of memories: those that daunt, those that don't. Memories are, basically, nothing more than "stuff" we think about. It's fairly common knowledge that memory formation involves strengthening of the synaptic connection between nerve cells. Studies show the synaptic connection is use-dependent. Therefore, when those connections between neurons aren't used often, they are eventually broken.

We access our knowledge banks to complete a task, to communicate in some way, whether verbally, by text, in facial or sign language. We rely on our memories to put together the simplest concepts. It would be next to impossible to function in our daily lives without the dependence upon memory. Why, then, is memory in its physical form, so mysterious, and even daunting? What sparks reaction to a person's emotional state when we connect with a specific memory? No one can refute the alterations that occur in personality once a memory is engaged in the brain.

Children are especially fascinating in their development of their memory banks. I marvel at their ease of retention. Their hunger for building good memories illuminates their precocious nature. Description of bad occurrences is emotion-filled, as most children will express their dislike for revisiting a distasteful experience.

But, children's minds are pliable. Unless, of course, you have an exceptional child, one who defies relativity – "the theory that space and time are relative concepts rather than absolute concepts." We can fashion little minds into believing what we, as adults, choose to expose them to. Once programmed, it is difficult to whitewash what has been brainwashed.

Unshackling the past and stepping into the present for me began with the Truth. Once I grew in the Truth, the process of ridding myself of haunting ghosts keeping me prisoner to my unpleasant history became a daily regimen. I had a head start in the process in that I hungered for this Truth as a child. I believe that hunger for the Truth is inbred. We don't know what it is we hunger for until the exposure. That's a stark reality of why it is incumbent upon parents to bring this Truth to their children. God commands it. *It is for this reason God commissioned us to go and tell the world. Missionaries feel that very urgent call to disclose Christ to those who have never had the opportunity to know Him.*

If I could have invented some sort of memory vice, my escape from prison would have been a much quicker process. *I'd also be a billionaire!* Who of us wouldn't like to extract the bad memories and leave the good? Just squeeze out the corrupted data from your head. Maybe just have automatic buttons with a built-in sensor to protect our memory bank from unwanted information: Reserve, Reject. Imagine the heartache we would be spared!

None of us need to escape the satisfying, gratifying part of life; nor do we want to. We prefer to hang onto the sweet memories. Those are the morsels of life that get us through future onslaughts of adversity. Oh, no, those we take pleasure in. Those add sweetness to our days. Throw me a crumb of a delightful memory and it can crowd out the unpleasant immediately.

The process of blocking out bad memories is not always a solo exercise. God equips others to aid in the progression. They are keepers of the keys for your prison doors. If – and there's another one of those key words – *if* you allow them rites of passage, it can accelerate your release from those chain-gang memories that keep you shackled to your prison of the past.

Webby: The Answer to My Love Prayer

Webby would hold one of the keys to my prison door. He was the keeper of a very important key for any young, hot-blooded, vibrant girl – the key to receiving *eros* love. God had begun preparing his heart – stitching it to mine – several years prior. Some time passed before God would darn the hole in my heart with the same thread used to darn Webby's congenital defect.

Now, you need to understand that I fell in love with Webby at first sight. There was no choice in the matter for me. It was completely orchestrated by God that our hearts would connect. Hindsight brings such clear vision. I was totally submissive to God's call in my life, without fully realizing at my tender age that I had relinquished my subservience to Him. He had become the navigator of my days. As cloudy as many of those times were, I surrendered their outcome to God.

My long-time high school sweetheart had invited me to visit his church. I had resisted every time, but finally gave in on this one occasion. There was a new youth minister in town and everyone was supposed to bring a friend. *What a mistake on his part!* One glance at Webby (*my little stud-man; he was so cute – all 120 pounds of him!*) and it was all over but the shoutin'. I was eighteen. I had been praying the send-someone-to-teach-me-how-to-love prayer since I was twelve. *Yes, I had not stopped even while dating my high school sweetie.* Webby was clearly the answer to my unceasing six-year prayer. *I knew it immediately. It would take a little time for God to break the news to Webby that he had an appointment with destiny.* I would break it off with my long-standing boyfriend and by the next year become Mrs. Webster Oglesby.

Walking into matrimony with absolutely no idea of what a real marriage resembled was going to be nothing short of a challenge. Not to mention I had lots of what we commonly refer to as "baggage" to drag along with me. Couple that with the extra pressure of being married to a youth minister … it would be quite amazing if I managed to pull off even pretending how to fashion a home.

The running of a household was a piece of cake. I'd managed a family of ten. There was nothing domesticated I wouldn't be able to handle. The hardest thing I had to deal with in that area was learning to cook for two rather than ten. *Webby teases me still today about my army-size cooking habits. That's probably when he developed a dislike for leftovers. We did have them for a while! We seldom had leftovers back at home.*

We only had two months to the day for me to wrap my mind around becoming a wife. Webby had come to realize home life for me was far from ideal. The first moment he recognized signs of physical abuse, he came to my rescue sooner than either of us anticipated. *Perhaps it was the long sleeves, turtleneck and long pants I wore in South Georgia in the extreme humid September heat that were the dead give-aways. I was moving rather delicately, as well. Remember, I was eighteen by now, but nothing much had changed on the homefront.* Little did I know that Webby was saving up for a ring. Accelerating the date meant it wouldn't grace my finger for seventeen years, but we were just as married without the engagement ring.

Yes, everyone had the same thought. It set the stage for some really juicy gossip in a small-town and the Methodist church where he ministered. But, our oldest daughter wouldn't come for almost three years into our marriage. *Long gestation!*

Can I Pull This Off?

Two months to the day of engagement? That's not much time for a bride-to-be to work with. The wedding ceremony was not my problem. I can handle organizational details in nothing flat. I had formal wedding announcements ordered and delivered in an Emily Post acceptable fashion. Webby and I drove to Jacksonville, Florida and made our purchases at May Cohen's Department Store. I purchased my wedding gown. A perfect fit. No alterations necessary. It was the only size zero they had; took it right off the mannequin and out the store it went with me. *I weighed all of 96 pounds the day I married. Oh, my. What time and birthing will do to a woman!* I selected and ordered eight bridesmaids' and one junior bridesmaid's dresses that would have to be custom made and shipped, made gift registry selections, ordered the cakes *(yes, even had a groom's cake),* and purchased our wedding bands all in a day's work. We purchased everything we needed to purchase and had a quite splendid wedding for $175. *Yes, times have really changed!* It was a blessing that his mother had worked in a florist shop, so she prepared all the flowers. My mother, bless her sweet heart, managed to meager-out money for the nuts and punch. She did all she could, and I was thrilled with her contribution.

No, the ceremony part was easy. It was other issues that concerned this gal. I did some mighty tall praying within that period of time. I dug into the scriptures, replenished my heart with the assurance of Paul that "I can do *everything* through Him who gives me strength." Over and over I would recite that assurance. I had to convince myself that I was worthy to receive God's answer to my prayer.

My biggest concern was how to explain to Webby that my virginity had been stolen from me. *That was still a big deal back then. It is rare today even to know a virgin, much less be one.* I had engaged in some heavy petting, but had never willingly given myself to anyone. Webby would be the first. But, how would I explain it? I certainly was not going to offer an explanation; that much I knew. I could only pray that he loved me enough to surmise whatever he chose, but should he ask, what then? The fear of rejection by the man I was deeply in love with was almost too much to bear. I wouldn't think about it. I couldn't. The outcome might be too painful. What if he wanted nothing to do with me? And, who could blame him for that? Who would want to marry damaged goods?

I had lost my virginity. That might serve to be a real stumbling block. I had no idea. But, I didn't *give* it away. It was stolen from me. I had no choice in the matter. I was but a child. So, I began to pray

~~~

Now, fix that God! You can't, can you? That's something that a young girl never gets again. You can't buy it. You can't manufacture it. You can't surgically put it back. You can't even dream it back. It's just gone! (Oh, my, I think I just found Dad's anger he misplaced!) Lord, take this hurt away. I'm confused. What if Webby doesn't want me when he finds out? With everything in me that feels like love, this is it. The agony gnaws at me day and night, Lord. I know what your Word says. I've read it, but ...

~~~

Do not fret because of evil men, or be envious of those who do wrong; for like the grass they will soon wither, Like green plants they will soon die away. Trust in the Lord and do good; dwell in the land and enjoy safe pasture. Delight yourself in the Lord., and he will give you the desires of your heart. Commit your way to the Lord Trust in him and he will do this: He will make your righteousness shine like the dawn, the justice of your cause like the noonday sun. Be still before the Lord and wait patiently for him; do not fret when men succeed in their ways, when they carry out their wicked schemes. Refrain from anger and turn from wrath; do not fret—it leads only to evil. For evil men will be cut off, but those who hope in the Lord will inherit the land. A little while, and the wicked will be no more; though you look for them, they will not be found. But the meek will inherit the land and enjoy great peace. The wicked plot against the righteous and gnash their teeth at them; but the Lord laughs at the wicked, for he knows their day is coming. The wicked draw the sword and bend the bow to bring down the poor and needy, to slay those whose ways are upright. But their swords will

> pierce their own hearts, and their bows will be broken. Better
> the little that the righteous have than the wealth of many
> wicked; for the power of the wicked will be broken, but the
> Lord upholds the righteous. The days of the blameless are
> known to the Lord, and their inheritance will endure forever.
>
> ~Psalm 37:1-18 (NIV)

~~~

… prepare his heart for me, O Lord.

~~~

Answered Prayer

God answered that prayer. He did prepare Webby's heart to receive me just the way I was. Broken. No questions asked. He just accepted me. And loved me. God is ever faithful to deliver. I was learning to accept the beauty behind trusting God. I was beginning to discover how much lighter my load was when I allowed Him to guide my path. But, I was not ready to allow Him full control over my decisions. I ignored confidence He rightfully deserved. I would hang onto the reservation about sharing my past with Webby. I wouldn't want to lose the gift God had sent me.

~~~

I often wonder had I not prayed for God's input into the selection of my husband, who would I have chosen? Would I have been the blessed woman I am? Would I have been drawn to someone like my dad, thinking I was not worthy of any better? Would I have "overlooked" the answered prayer when it was right before my eyes? Would I have been bold enough to pursue my dream had I not been equipped with the strength of Christ? I shutter at the thought.

~~~

117

Keeping Secrets

Mum would be the word. I continued to struggle with the thought. It wouldn't be as though I would be lying to Webby by not telling him. I just wouldn't offer the truth unless questioned. He didn't. I was grateful for the privacy. It would serve everyone concerned best to remain silent. The silent sin that occurred in my life would remain a secret. Only God, myself, and the ones who had robbed me of my initiation into womanhood would know. They weren't talking, and I certainly would not.

~~~

How disturbing that Satan has robbed our young girls of the desire for the blessing of purity. Man's sexual perversion is relentless. Sexual desire was created not only for procreation purposes, but also for the element of pleasure. But, God gifted it to each of us along with an ample dose of self-control. His standards for sexual purity are clearly defined in His Word.

~~~

But among you there must not be even a hint of sexual immorality, or of any kind of impurity, or of greed, because these are improper for God's holy people. Nor should there be obscenity, foolish talk or coarse joking, which are out of place, but rather thanksgiving. For of this you can be sure: no immoral, impure or greedy person—such a man is an idolater—has any inheritance in the kingdom of Christ and of God. Let no one deceive you with empty words, for because of such things God's wrath comes on those who are disobedient. Therefore, do not be partners with them.

~Ephesians5:3-7 (NIV)

~~~

Fathers, love your daughters and teach them about the ways of men. Give them insight to a man's thoughts. Tell her what a man will say to her in order to get her to perform sexually. Inform her of how a man looks at her once he's conquered her; she no longer will be a challenge to him. Talk straight and mince no words. Spare her, nor yourself, no embarrassment. She may be your baby girl, but she is a woman to someone else.

Likewise, teach your sons to respect their bodies as well as a young girl's. I am often surprised when I hear out of the mouths of Christian men these words about their sons: "Ah, they're going to sew their wild oats," or "Boys will be boys." God expects sexual purity from your son as much as He does a young girl. God expects self-control from your son. And, God expects you to be the spiritual provider within your home that offers godly wisdom and instruction to your son, not excuses for his maleness. Teach him common courtesy; it covers a lot of territory. He will mimic your example.

~~~

> Train a child in the way he should go, and
> when he is old he will not turn from it.
>
> ~ Proverbs 22:6 (NIV)

~~~

Mothers, dress your daughter appropriately. You are the keeper of the funds, or at least should have some say in how she spends her allotment. You are her voice of approval. You set the standard by the way you dress. She's your daughter. Dress her provocatively, allow her to select stimulating apparel, and you are offering her as a sacrifice to a force to be reckoned with. You understand womanhood. You also understand the driving force of a man. Teach her self-control. Drill in her to love her body, for when we love, we protect. Teach her abortion is not an option. Birth control is not an invitation to promiscuous behavior. You are her guardian. She is **your** *baby. She doesn't need one herself until she's in a covenant relationship.*

Set boundaries early for your son. Teach him to be considerate and respectful of others. You are a woman, so teach him the ways of women — how we manipulate, stimulate, and activate man's senses. Make him aware of how women seduce the mind. Give him tools to equip him on how to respond to such untoward invitations.

Parents, you have but one chance to keep their hearts, minds and bodies pure and spotless before the Lord. The responsibility rests on your shoulders for a short while. You have been called to a high position. Don't miss it. Instruct them in the ways of the Lord. Don't predispose them to a prison of recklessness, comparisons, venereal diseases, dealing with the guilt of abortion, and a tainted marital bed. You do your job. The rest is up to them.

~~~

> Discipline your children, for in that there is hope;
>
> do not be a willing party to their death.
>
> ~Proverbs 19:18 (NIV)

~~~

God would continue to reveal truths and consoling wisdom. Webby and I would grow in love and in spiritual depth. We were young. I was a fresh out-of-the-gate 19, and he was a few days shy of 24 on the day we wed. There was much I loved about him, but his passion for the Lord was awe-inspiring. He would prove to be a great vessel for my escape from the past, and my arrival into the present.

18

Part 2: Fugitive in the Present

Learning to Trust

Brides are typically charged with many responsibilities in preparation for a wedding. I had two months to the day – October 4th to December 4th – to get everything done. Sandwiched between the arrangements for a ceremony was preparing my heart for allowing a man to seek my trust. He had already invaded my senses. Outside of my high school relationship, I had no idea what other men were like. *My high school flame was very much the gentleman to me. He never yelled or was belligerent in any manner. He always respected me and did his best to make me happy. I was easy to love, but hard to conquer. I often wondered if he understood the gravity of my reservation of men. Having helped us out on the farm occasionally, he had been eyewitness to my dad's temper. I don't believe he ever knew the magnitude of what I went through in my home. He did encourage me to elope several times. I'm sure it was in part to protect me. He had a great heart.*

~~~

So, here I was. Two months away from marrying the man I had fallen in love with immediately, and one whom I had spent the last year of my life convincing that he was supposed to fall in love with me *(Webby says I chased him till he caught me)*, but I had a more gripping issue than the but-I'm-not-a-virgin issue that I had to deal with. Trust. Would I ever be able to trust a man? What if I burned breakfast? How angry would he get? Do all husbands beat their wives? Do they all yell and curse at their spouses? Does every man belittle and demean his mate? How would I react to his touch? Would it be different somehow from what I had known? Would it be special? How will I respond to his love? Was this really something I could handle emotionally?

Consequently, I found myself back on my knees. *Help me, Lord, I pray. Make me pure. Make me whole. Make me a worthy bride. Don't let me mess this up. I love him, Lord. You sent him to me. Help me protect your gift of love to me.*

It was enough to make a girl crazy. I felt caught up in some soap opera: "As the Stomach Churns!" I wanted this more than anything, yet it could well be the very death of me. And, if it didn't resolve itself in my mind quickly, death might be sooner than later! This was a serious matter.

The man I was to marry would be a keeper of the keys to unlock different chambers in my heart. Little did I know how many keys he would hold. I was stepping out of prison, but I suddenly realized, I would only be a fugitive to my present.

I had bought a new Bible. Its pages were not as familiar to my touch. No prominent markings. No turned-down corners. No underscorings. Just new, crisp pages I'd have to become accustomed. *My dad burned my Gideons' Bible along with my clothes when he learned Webby and I were engaged. I didn't tell him for two weeks. I never allowed Webby to go to him to "ask for my hand." He suspected there was little reason to ask Dad for my hand; he just didn't understand why.*

Navigating the new Bible was like wearing a new pair of shoes – trying to break in the leather, seeking a nice, comfortable fit. It served the same purpose, whether new or old; just getting into the groove of the "new" took a few uses.

I coursed through some of my cornerstone verses. Ephesians 1:13-14 (NIV) was a reminder of Whose I was, and that assurance calmed my fears.

~~~

And you also were included in Christ when you

Heard the word of truth, the gospel of your salvation.

Having believed, you were marked in him with a seal,

the promised Holy Spirit, who is a deposit guaranteeing

Our inheritance until the redemption of those who are

God's possession—to the praise of his glory.

~~~

"I" had been marked in Him with a seal! That seal was the promised Holy Spirit. That was my Comfort that had been dwelling inside me since that day by the mantel. It was the Holy Spirit's hands on my shoulders as I cried out in agony on my knees at the foot of the fireplace. He had marched into my prison that day. He was a plant; sneaking in through the Word. He had become my cellmate. He would partner with me and mastermind a plan to step out of this prison together. He would not leave me. We were a pair – the Encourager and lil' ol' frightened me; the Mighty One and weak me; the Keeper of "the" Key and locked-up me. God would send others who would unlock certain chambers in my heart. With their help, I would advance from Cell Block A to B and C. But until I could step out of the prison of my past, I would not walk with the Light on my face.

~~~

God often sends others as profound influences in our lives. When we adopt a relationship with godly men and women, we open our lives for cultivating the wisdom of God. They have life's experiences that have seasoned their steps. The fruits of the Holy Spirit exemplified in their lives bear witness to the sound principles found in God's Word and serve to attest to God's character.

Opening your life to fellow Christians doesn't necessarily mean they will be a positive influence in your life. Some will disappoint you. Some will hurt you. Take precaution for the godly wisdom you gain from others. Whereas none of us is perfect, look for spiritual maturity in a person whose counsel you seek. Age doesn't always accompany spiritual maturity. It's often the hardships and trials someone has suffered that bring the lessons in life.

~~~

Developing Trust

Trust. It's a rich word. Its meaning: "faith, belief, hope, conviction, confidence, expectation, reliance and dependence." Wow! How do you develop a relationship with someone who may or may not come through for you with the values that trust offers? If you've been hurt deeply by someone, it's a difficult point to reach again.

Having developed a trust in the Lord helped me. Developing a rich and powerful prayer life was most beneficial. Praying for wisdom and discernment in situations is useful, as well. Asking for protection and deliverance is not out of the question. God hears us, but then we must trust Him to place people in our lives of whom we can trust, as well. We may never experience complete freedom if we fail to develop trust.

~~~

My son, preserve sound judgment and discernment, do not let them out of your sight; they will be life for you, an ornament to grace your neck.

Then you will go on your way in safety, and your foot will not stumble; when you lie down, you will not be afraid; when you lie down, your sleep will be sweet.

Have no fear of sudden disaster or of the ruin that overtakes the wicked, for the LORD will be your confidence and will keep your foot from being snared.

~Proverbs 3:21-26 (NIV)

~~~

My release date had been announced. It would be December 4th, 1971. I was on a journey with this Holy Spirit dwelling inside me. He would offer me wisdom, and courage and strength to succeed. He had already met my every need in order to endure years of hardship at home. This path couldn't be any more difficult than the road I had traversed. It would be different. I was determined it would be different. There would be much to learn, but I had resolved to set my mind to discover all the ways love and home and family could be different. I would break the chain of the legacy that I was emerging from. Together, the three of us – God, Webby, and I – would make a history, a new legacy, and one that would be pleasing to God. I could do this. Not of my own power, but through God I could do this.

It called to mind another of my favorite passages of scripture. It is a message from God's Word that I would use often throughout my life. The ancient words inscribed on pages for countless others to draw strength, courage and wisdom from would speak to me with new and vibrant acumen. *I rely on it still today.*

~~~

> I rejoiced greatly in the Lord that at last you renewed your concern for me. Indeed, you were concerned, but you had no opportunity to show it. I am not saying this because I am in need, for I have learned to be content whatever the circumstances. I know what it is to be in need, and I know what it is to have plenty. I have learned the secret of being content in any and every situation, whether well fed or hungry, whether living in plenty or in want. I can do all this through him who gives me strength.
>
> ~Philippians 4:10-13

~~~

Reconciled Spirit

My spirit was finally reconciled. God would not have brought this answer to my love prayer in order to cause me harm. His assurance was that He would protect me. Perhaps I wouldn't develop ulcers from thinking about how I would pull this whole marriage bit off. It would be a gradual course. I would learn to trust this man God had sent to me. I had experienced the sense of how trust felt, the rewards of allowing someone to protect me. Until I had reason not to trust, I would not allow walls around my heart to keep out this man of God. He felt comfortable. He reflected the life of Christ. I would follow the inclination to fling open the door of my heart and learn to love with fervor. What I didn't know, I would fashion my heart to receive. I would approach this new life in the manner I had the one I was exiting – one day at a time.

~~~

19

Part 2: Fugitive in the Present

Are My Stripes Showing?

Realization had set in. I had dressed in my there's-a-new-girl-in-town attire. I was feeling sassy. Stepping high. But something was slipping. I felt it every now and again. I finally stopped to assess the situation. There it was, shining like a slip hanging lower than a skirt hem – my prison garb! I had on this beautiful new garment labeled "Christian, Designed by God," and here were these striped prison garments exposed! I thought I had concealed them, covered up the shame, the guilt, and the pain from my past.

God had seen me through this trying stretch in this race of life. I had made it. I was a survivor, an overcomer. Webby was my ticket home. God had answered my prayer, and I was supposed to live happily ever after. Wasn't that the way it should be? But how do you get out of prison and still wear the stripes? I wasn't in my prison home any longer. I worried that if the prison uniform was visible to me, everyone else could see it, too.

I feared my inadequacies would show. My failures. My weaknesses. I'm a pretty transparent kind of person. I don't hide my feelings well. Oh, I could mask unpleasant shameful, painful experiences, but to be ill-prepared or incompetent in some task, I don't know; that just didn't sound too appealing. It was a test, and I never tested well in school. I hated tests. I got nervous, totally unsure of myself for fear I would fall short. I didn't like failure. But, this test was a really big one. This was a marriage, and God took marriages very seriously.

If I failed at this, then what? Where would I go? Never back home, that was for certain. I could make it. I was a survivor. God would team up with me, and with Him on my side I could survive anything.

~~~

There I was … gripped with fear. I wasn't lacking confidence in myself. I was questioning my confidence in God! Stepping out of prison, but a fugitive. I was continually looking over my shoulder at the negatives planted in my head by my parents and teachers, the naysayers in my life. Fear is a stumbling block for overcoming past, present or future encumbrances. It can stifle progress. It can block out God's wisdom in a life. Fear interferes with relationships – with God and others. Fear distracts from the blessings that come in trusting God's adequacy for our lives.

How do you know when the way is clear and you need not fear? Developing that intimacy with God. Feeling His hand of assurance on your shoulder and knowing it is the Holy Spirit's protection of you. There is a gentleness of your spirit that settles on your heart and calms your fear. His love envelops you. You will know when God's hand has arrested the uncertainty that clouds your thinking. Study the Word, seek His wisdom, and expect His intervention. It will come.

~~~

> This is how love is made complete among us so that we will have confidence on the day of judgment: In this world we are like Jesus. There is no fear in love. But perfect love drives out fear, because fear has to do with punishment. The one who fears is not made perfect in love.
>
> We love because he first loved us.
>
> ~I John 4:17-19 (NIV)

~~~

God's Counsel

Seeking God's counsel would be essential if I was going to build a home, and especially one different from what I had known. The uncertainty of what "home" should look like was frightening to me. I confided in a close Christian friend that I felt inept at knowing how to go about establishing a life with someone else. Tina was tender and compassionate. But, she confided in me at the time that she was not one to be asking about how to make a man happy. She and her husband would be filing for divorce soon. *What! As though I needed to hear about that just now!*

I knew how to present petitions to God. I was confident He was a come-through God. But, was I a come-through gal? My biggest problem was, I didn't even know what to ask for. The only roadmap I had was full of dead-end streets. Those that didn't dead end headed off the deep end.

So, what now? Could I just ask God to supply whatever it was I needed? Yep, I could. But, I'm a gal of specifics. I like getting down and dotting i's and crossing t's. I took Him at His word when He said:

~~~

> Let your gentleness be evident to all. The Lord is near. Do not
> be anxious about anything, but in every situation, by prayer and
> petition, with thanksgiving, present your requests to God. And
> the peace of God, which transcends all understanding, will
> guard your hearts and your minds in Christ Jesus.
>
> ~Philippians 4:5-7 (NIV)

~~~

I believe in coming boldly to God and asking Him specifically for what I need, detail by detail. Nothing is impossible for Him. He knows my need before I ask, but He desires that I come to His throne. I knew enough about Him to understand He was a jealous God – with our time, with our praise, and with our worship. I knew He was a God who stood behind His promises. I knew there was no situation in which I would be involved that He wouldn't show up if I asked Him to. *And even without invitation.* I had put Him to the test many times.

So, in my two-month crunch of time, there would definitely be a lot of God in the picture. Yes, I could pull this thing off, but only if God was on board with me. Marrying a man whose heart sought after the Lord was a pretty good start for a woman who knew nothing about making a house a home. So, ready or not, I plunged forward.

Guilty by Default

The chain of guilt is a strong one. It is also one that gives no wriggle room. You won't go far from the place it shackled you, because guilt is stingy with its links. It wants you to stay close in proximity to the "scene of the crime." That way, guilt can keep an eye on you. After all, when eyes are on you, it's off of the responsible party.

Regardless of whether you've been the victim of physical, emotional, sexual or spiritual abuse, you can become guilt-ridden. A divorce situation in which you had no control, no decision, no desire to be involved in can leave you guilty by default. Any relationship gone sour and left unresolved can plague you with remorse for what could/should have been. Most problematic relationships involve the fault of both parties. Typically, no one person is to blame, though that is not always the situation.

~~~

In abuse situations involving children, the children often blame themselves. Because they are especially vulnerable and trusting, it's difficult for children to distinguish between "I did something bad" or "Somebody did something bad to me." When a child is told he/she is bad, good for nothing, or no one else will love him/her, it's easy to feel abuse is deserved. The feelings of guilt become even stronger. Those thoughts entered my thinking often as a young unassuming child.

I believe my mother shared some of these same feelings. Though she never verbalized her thought process, she seemed to display a sense that she deserved what was happening to her.

No one deserves maltreatment. Sin is the root of defeat in many innocent lives. Oh, how we squander God's richest resources. When we are shackled to the links of guilt, we feel unworthy to serve, to love, to share intimate, meaningful relationships with others. But, most of all, it hog-ties us from enjoying an up-close-and-personal relationship with our Lord. Satan's hold on the army of Christians is debilitating the furtherance of God's Kingdom. There are other strongholds preventing Kingdom growth, like selfishness and worldly distractions, but certainly being shackled to past guilt is among the list.

~~~

God desires we be relieved of any guilt that keeps us at bay from knowing Him more intimately. Whether our guilt stems from sin we committed or someone committed against us, if we are a child of the King, that guilt has been transferred to Him. You no longer must be hostage to shameful acts inflicted by you or upon you. Unlock that shackle! It's over, Baby! That key is a given.

Regaining Self-Confidence

Other issues would present themselves. I had little encouragement to boost my self-confidence throughout the years. The last six weeks of my senior year in high school was the most encouraging time of my childhood. College interns would be our instructors. They were new blood. Not from around our parts. They knew nothing of my family, didn't judge a book by its cover, and looked strictly at a student's potential. I was fortunate to have a sneak preview of what the world might look like on the other side of despair. Throughout my high school courses of study, I had received some encouragement from only two teachers – my typing and English instructors, but never a challenge to reach my potential. These interns spawned a dynamic in me that had long been suppressed by my parents. For years I'd endured hurting words such as, "You're not smart enough to figure that out," and "You'll never amount to a hill of beans" *(my dad's favorite putdown)*, and "Beauty is only skin deep anyway, so don't worry that you were born ugly."

It's enough to shatter a young girl's self-confidence. And, it did. I had a mixture of lack of self-confidence with a strong self-determination. It was a good balance; enough to keep me from fading into a world of hopelessness. Had I not been fortunate enough to steady the scales between the two, I wonder where my path would have taken me. I believe God gives each of us a special gift, a measure in character that brings us to a place to find our strength. We must will it for ourselves. I didn't sit on my will. I exercised it.

I continued to seek God's favor. It's a funny thing, you know. When we search, we may find the exact thing we're looking for. We may even uncover other misplaced treasures along the way. Then, there are those times we never find what it is for which we're searching, but we manage to live without it. God was beginning to reveal to me lessons of what I felt I had lost in my past. There's typically a lesson behind misplaced, found, or lost forever. Once the answer comes, it's important to find the lesson in the answer and then to tuck it away for future use. You can be certain the character God is building within you will be put to the test again.

~~~

I believed my dad had misplaced anger. Or, was it? His father had bequeathed it to him. Then, Dad would share it with his wife and eight children, and will it to his sons. Some of them would use it for a while and pass it on to their family additions.

The reality is ... it wasn't misplaced at all. The stories that would originate from the family history would be evidence of how his misplaced anger was not only found, but also planted in generational seeds producing fruits of resentment, bitterness, jealousy, divisiveness and abomination.

Despite all the unsettling emotions in the family, there was still a bond that would filter through the siblings and numerous offspring. At least there was a desire to bond by some in the heritage. Estrangement does have a way of erecting barriers warding off any restoration of separation. Fighting to overcome the spoiled fruits is difficult. Individuals have to begin with their immediate family and make a change in the legacy at that branch of the tree.

~~~

Reestablishing Self-Worth

I had a lot of "self" issues I was beginning to realize had been misplaced in my life. Self-worth was another. *Where did it go? It's got to be here somewhere.* Someone else had stripped me of it when I was younger. Who would want to take something so valuable from a person? It's like panties – so personal. Why, those people came equipped with their own share of self-worth, didn't they?

~~~

The moment I focused on self-worth, it took me back to the past again. There I was, standing in front of Ms. Franklin, my fourth-grade teacher. I could hear her squawking at me still.

"Nobody wants to sit near you. You smell. You're foul. I want you to sit in the back of the room and never come up to the front of the class. Don't ask to go out during class. Don't raise your hand, because when you move, you stir up the air. Just sit and don't breathe with your mouth open. I want you to go home and bathe, and –"

"But, Ms. Franklin, I'm not allowed—"

"Shut up. I don't want you to say a word, do you hear me? Just do what I tell you to do. Take a bath. Why do you smell anyway? Don't you ever...?"

"Ms. Franklin, I can't help..."

"I said shut up. Get back in that classroom and just sit. And don't come back in here if you can't get something else to wear."

Ms. Franklin never allowed me to say a word. Had she listened to my heart, I could have told her all the reasons I smelled. I was a bed-wetter. It wouldn't have been hard to figure why I was had she realized how disrupted my nights were. Had she asked, I would have told her how my mother was so determined to break me from the disgusting habit that she would rub my nose in the urine-stained bed each morning before school. Failing to break me of my weakness, she would bend me over the bed with my nose in the urine and give me a good whoopin' with a round curtain rod. Weeks would pass with no improvement. She then refused to allow me to bathe until I broke the dreadful habit.

Had she only allowed me to answer when she asked, I could have explained my condition. It would be only one instance of being close to rescue. People's intolerance of underlying circumstances in others' lives can strip away important virtues like self-worth, self-confidence, and self-motivation. They get replaced with things like self-denial, self-defeating, and self-deprecating.

~~~

Now, to find that self-worth of mine. I know it was here somewhere. I could plunder around in my soul looking for it. It would be like a scavenger hunt. But, find it I would. The Holy Spirit was leaning heavy in my ear, bidding me along my way. I'd keep looking. Surely it would turn up somewhere.

~~~

> When the Sadducees were challenging Jesus regarding the greatest of the commandments, Jesus' reply was simple and swift: "The most important one," answered Jesus, "is this: 'Hear, O Israel, the Lord, our God, the Lord is one. Love the Lord your God with all your heart and with all your soul and with all your mind and with all your strength. The second is this: Love your neighbor as yourself. There is no commandment greater than these." ~Mark 12:28-31 (NIV)

~ ~ ~

Love God, then others as yourself. No one in his/her right mind wishes harm on him/herself. Nor does God. He desires we all be loved – healthily, heartily, and habitually. We are valuable in God's sight. Value equals worth. I reflected on this and other scripture verses time and time again. In order to regain my "selfs" that I had lost, I could no longer be a fugitive in the present.

It would be mind over matter. I would have to renew my mind. It would take – here we go again with one of those "self" words – self-control. I could think my way into a better way of acting. Upon reflection, I had been in that mindset even in my childhood by focusing on my anchor verse of Philippians 4:8.

Charles Stanley in his book, *A Touch of His Wisdom*, has this to say about controlling your thoughts:

> "The key to developing self-control with a spiritual emphasis is not more self-determination. It is not a doubling of efforts or better time management. The pivotal discipline for gaining godly self-control is the renewing of the mind. Like the ancient walls, the mind is the crucial defense mechanism. If it is broached by negative, critical, undisciplined thoughts, our behavior and our entire personality are adversely affected. We act out the way we perceive ourselves, the way we think. Our actions conform with our thinking. Right thinking is the first step toward right living."[1]

I would wrap my thoughts around, again, my banner verse – "Whatever is true, right, pure, noble, lovely, admirable, praiseworthy, and excellent" (Phil. 4:8). Seeing all those qualities in me – *yes, as God created me with these virtues* – would restore my self-worth.

Oh, there you are! I found you. Where have you been, my long lost friend? It was there all along. It had just gotten buried beneath a pile of rubble. I hadn't worn it in so long, now that I had grown, it wasn't exactly the right fit. Either I had to downsize, or it had to upsize. I wasn't quite certain how to slip back into it. For now, it

---

[1] Stanley, Dr. Charles, *A Touch of His Freedom*, JAMC, May 10, 2005, 1 72 (10), 12.

would just be a little snug, a bit uncomfortable to show off, but in time and with love, the luster would be restored to this once misplaced virtue.

Again, I would have to give time time. I would have to incorporate another dose of patience as I waited on God to fix me. And Webby. He was in the mix now. He would wait on me and help fix me. He wouldn't run ahead of me, or leave me stranded while I was finding myself in this new life. God knew who to pair with me – my own handpicked selection by God. What a patient man this husband of mine has always been.

I would reclaim and fully restore my self-worth. Suppressing those reminders would be a part of that process. I developed a habit of exchanging the sour-tasting thoughts for more pleasant ones instead. Webby was my source for good memories. I was slowly emptying out the bad in order to make room for the good ones he would help create.

~~~

Another reason God paired us. That's when you know you complement one another. You draw from each other's strengths. You don't point out your spouse's weaknesses; you simply make up for them. You support one another's efforts. You become a team. You patiently wait for him or her to catch up when he or she falls behind. You run to catch up if he or she gets ahead. You finish the race together. You can pass the baton for a stint, but catch your breath because you're the next leg. You meet needs, whatever they are. You protect. You mend wounds. Apply healing ointment, not vinegar. You love – when you feel like it, and when you don't; when your spouse is happy or when grumpy. You still and always love. And wait. And pray. You hold your mate up in constant prayer for God's favor in his or her life. You ask for protection of the mind, body and soul. You speak wisely and show respect. And give time time. Your spouse may be healing from the past. You will be an important key in the process.

~~~

If I speak in the tongues of men and of angels, but have not love, I am only a resounding gong or a clanging cymbal. If I have the gift of prophecy and can fathom all mysteries and all knowledge, and if I have a faith that can move mountains, but have not love, I am nothing. If I give all I possess to the Poor

and surrender my body to the flames, but have not love, I gain
nothing. Love is patient, love is kind. It does not envy, it does
not boast, it is not proud. It is not rude, it is not self-seeking, it
is not easily angered, it keeps no record of wrongs. Love does
not delight in evil but rejoices with the truth. It always protects,
always trusts, always hopes, always perseveres. Love never fails.
But where there are prophecies, they will cease; where there are
tongues, they will be stilled; where there is knowledge, it will
pass away. For we know in part and we prophesy in part, but
when perfection comes, the imperfect disappears. When I was a
child, I talked like a child, I thought like a child, I reasoned like
a child. When I became a man, I put childish ways behind me.
Now we see but a poor reflection as in a mirror; then we shall
see face to face. Now I know in part; then I shall know fully,
even as I am fully known. And now these three remain: faith,
hope and love. But the greatest of these is love.

~I Corinthians 13 (NIV)

~ ~ ~

I had stepped out of prison, but I would remain a fugitive
for a few years. The past would constantly bear down my back. I'd
glance over my shoulder to see if it was catching up. It stayed close
on my trail. It took a lot of effort for me to rebuild some of the
values that had been mislaid in my brief years on this earth. It
would have been simpler to overcome the past if my new world had
consisted of the three of us – God, Webby and me. But, alas, there
would be others in the mix. The Garden of Eden would become
crowded, making life and keeping the past at bay more difficult.

> *Fear distracts from the blessings that come in trusting God's adequacy for our lives.*

20

Part 2: Fugitive in the Present

Getting Rid of the Evidence

In a different environment, I was beginning to green-up. Coming to life was exciting. Experiencing a daily dose of love was new. Waking up to "I love you," being reassured repeatedly throughout the day that I was loved, and hearing it before I fell asleep each night was nourishing my once-lifeless heart. Blossoming and flourishing wouldn't come for a while. I was transitioning into someone I never knew existed.

Or, did I? The poor gal had been suppressed for such a long time. Each time she would begin to spring forth, someone would put a lid on her head!

There was always someone around when I'd try to drag the jewel out of her box — a family member, a teacher, a classmate. I just couldn't seem to eject the real person. I worried she might suffocate down under. She never came up for air. There was a long time I never saw her even peek out. I thought I'd lost her forever! It was quite a relief to know she had just been hibernating.

Occasionally, someone would bring her out. The opportunity would present itself. Circumstances were perfect. Her personality just sparkled. She was actually having fun. Enjoying life. Caught up in the moment. And then ... some killjoy would come along, and back in the box she'd go. Blast-it! I kind of like that gal, too!

I finally got it!

Reestablishing my self-confidence and self-worth was yet another fundamental step in this process of getting past the past. Understanding my worth, not only as an individual and wife, but also to God allowed me to deal with life's obstacles in a positive way. I had an inheritance from God! The psalmist's words kept coursing through my mind ... *the blameless are known to the Lord, ... the blameless are known to the Lord ... the blameless ... and their inheritance will endure forever!* It was resonating now. It became abundantly clear to me that I was a product of redemption. I had been rescued from a cesspool of hatred, anger, and immorality, sin at its worst, none of which was my fault. I finally got it! None of the despicable injustices that had stolen my childhood were my fault.

That was the revelation. How I wish someone had explained that to me earlier in life. Anyone. A counselor at school. One of the neighbors who knew what was going on in our household. The doctor who allowed me to walk out of his office as a first-grader without intervention. Someone in law enforcement.

~~~

Oh, yeah, they came. Right up to our door. But rather than enforce the law, they'd sit in their patrol car and pass the liquor bottle to my dad, then send him back in to "behave himself." He didn't. I was the culprit who called the law every time, so I incurred his wrath. With a little more liquor and a lot more anger once he walked through the door, everything started all over again.

Anyone can be an advocate for a child in an abusive situation. It takes boldness, compassion, and action. Imagine how many children's souls could be changed if one voice would just speak up.

~~~

What anxiety could have been spared on my part had someone whispered in my ear, "Joyce, this is not your fault." This child beat herself up mentally. I blamed myself for whatever wrong befell me. I actually convinced myself I deserved everything bad that happened.

It doesn't matter if you grew up in a household like mine, worse than mine, or the extreme — something serene and pleasant. *Are there actually homes like that?* Many people have some "thing" that haunts — something that makes one possibly feel like he/she could never measure up to acceptance. He/she could never be good enough, smart enough, pretty enough, or worthy enough. The danger comes when someone starts believing all of the lies. Self-confidence is destroyed. Self-image is trodden down. Someone manages to convince him/her somewhere along the way — and it may have been of one's own doing — that he/she has nothing to offer, is a failure, weak, has shortcomings, is a hand-me-downer, just damaged goods.

When you're trying to break free from being a prisoner to a past or a fugitive in the present, there are a few things you must keep in mind. We're going to explore the process. Whereas I believe all things are possible through Jesus Christ, it is difficult to go cold-turkey in setting oneself free. It doesn't happen instantly. There are certain exercises you must do — an evaluation of sorts, and then other drills (like those I've already presented) that you'll incorporate into the process of stepping out of your prison. Let's explore a few.

1) Some things are not your fault.

Many of the haunting, daunting ghosts that follow you around and keep you a prisoner to a troubled mind may not have been of your own doing. You know who they are. You perhaps haven't shared them with anyone. I didn't for many, many years. But, these guys are your "bedfellers!" They rob you of your sleep, your peace, your tranquility, and your joy in life. You're very familiar with who they are. Their memory lingers and has actually burrowed inside the recesses of your recall, and when you least expect a visit from them, they pop in like an uninvited guest. It can just irritate the daylights out of you! It disrupts your day, your night, and your countenance. It puts you in a bad mood so that you're snappy to your spouse or family or friends. You become withdrawn, maybe even depressed, and no one knows why. And *you're* certainly not going to tell. If you had known how this one incident would plague you, you would've done whatever it took to prevent it!

But, doggone it, you can only control what's within your power to control. As a child, I was powerless to battle the forces over me. I was a victim to unrest, born into a home devoid of love, reared under the roof of parents who were not honoring God in their lives, and existing in a community that turned a deaf ear and a blind eye to what should have been addressed. I should have been rescued by an adult – any adult -- and wasn't. It was all out of my control. *That's why kids need advocates! Their voices don't always count.*

Sometimes choices are not ours, but the consequences are. Poor judgment, inappropriate behavior, mean-spirited and unrighteous actions by others can clog up our world. The physical scars from the striking blow of a swift fist or belt buckle don't run as deeply as the scars of a wounded spirit. Words slice much deeper. Our hearts are then left to sort through messages of dejection and rejection. It doesn't take a family member to damage or even destroy the vibrant spirit God placed in all of us – the spirit to be alive, wanted, accepted, desired, and loved. Sometimes, a mere stranger can break that spirit. But, these desires are feelings we all long for. These are feelings we all need to exist in a dog-eat-dog world.

Sometimes it's an unintentional rejection on the part of our parents; we make it such. Sibling rivalry can take hold. Feeling like we're in competition for attention of a parent, spouse, friend, co-worker, employer, or even sometimes your children can make you feel forsaken. This is especially true with little girls and their dads. Girls will always need to be "daddy's little princess," always win Dad's affection, attention, admiration, and loyalty. Fathers mark their daughters for life. Make sure yours is the mark of acceptance. Your daughter is going to seek it from someone. *Women hunger for acceptance, don't we? Love gone sour wounds our spirit. Betrayal from a man we love is penetrating. Working our way back to trust again is a very difficult process.*

Once we understand that some things are not our fault, we then can begin to recapture an air of self-worth and confidence. There will be steps to take beyond releasing ourselves from the guilt of feeling we were responsible. We will work through the process. But this is a great beginning to step out of a burdensome past.

2) Take Responsibility for Your Mistakes

We can't control others' actions; we can only control ours. Our control includes how we accept the consequences of someone else's wrongs against us.

But not everything that goes wrong in your life is someone else's fault. At some point in your life, you must be accountable for your actions. That is the second step in the process: taking responsibility for your mistakes.

Sometimes we make unwise choices. We exercise poor judgment. Perhaps we didn't commit a matter to prayer and then trust God to take care of it for us and patiently wait on His wisdom. Instead, we acted hastily. It "felt right," so we did it. Been guilty of that? You betcha. We've all been there. Some baggage we're dragging around is a direct result of when we were outside of our walk with God, yet we must still deal with the consequences in our Christian lives today. Abortion, out-of-wedlock pregnancy, an STD you contracted through immoral sexual behavior, gambling debts, harshly spoken words, a lapsed promise? Oh, the list of self-inflicted agonies can be very, very long, and it takes a mature Christian to look in the mirror and say, "I can't pass the buck this time. I really messed up, and I need to take my lumps, learn my lesson, make amends, and move on with life.

~~~

If one of your past mistakes was divorce, then you know that it's always the kids who suffer most. We shuffle them around, push them aside, pretend they're not in the decision to divide the family. After all, they're just kids. These are adult matters. The youngsters just don't know all the circumstances involved. They shouldn't. But what happens to them in the aftermath? "Oh, kids are resilient. They bounce back." That's the school of thought. Don't fool yourself. Children never bounce back from being separated from a parent. They only bounce from house to house. Whose weekend is it? Who gets them at Christmas this year? What about Thanksgiving? Summer vacation?

"Who's going to buy my school supplies, Mommy?"

"Your daddy is in charge of that. Talk to him."

"Daddy had a girlfriend over, Mommy. She's nice."

Your heart melts. The war games are on. Your boyfriend comes home with you. Now there are four in the mix. The child has to be careful what she says about Mommy to Daddy and Daddy to Mommy. Parents pit the children against one another, and then kids are left with the guilt of what they said wrong. Yeah, they're resilient. They bounce back. Back and forth, back and forth, back and forth.

It's a constant battle of love-hate. The love you hate you left behind. Or, is it you hate the love you left behind? Confusing? Didn't I just say the same thing? Not really. It's all in the way you say it. But, I'll restate it if you'd like. The love you hate, you left behind. There, is that better? Needed the pause there, didn't it? Perhaps if the "pause" had been there before things got out of hand, the kids wouldn't still be bouncing. Something to think about.

~~~

Sometimes guilt prevails after the death of someone who was very special to you. There was a problem between the two of you that never got resolved. You're left with no closure and feelings of lingering guilt.

It could be a bad financial decision that haunts you. I've certainly made some of those. Some have been made for me, like in our recent economic downturn. It can take a long time to recover from a financial crunch, but we have to keep plugging away.

Don't allow unwelcome consequences from poor judgment to enslave you. Dwelling on them only keeps you hostage to your mistakes. Squeeze all the wisdom you can from past lessons and apply the experience to the future. Something similar is bound to present itself again. Or, your life lesson may also be used to help someone in the same predicament. That's when you know God has worked a great number on your life — when you are a vessel for others' healing.

3) You Can't Change a Thing

Not one day, one hour, one moment can you redial in order to relive. Regardless of what's been said, history does not repeat itself. It may come close, but it can never be duplicated to its preciseness once lived. *God's divine works of woven history always fascinate me. Webby's parents met and wed in the exact same location he and I met and wed twenty-nine years later. Mrs. Oglesby's house was located on the lot where the Methodist Church set, the same spot where Webby and I met and married. Amazing!*

Even if we come close to replicating history, we don't always learn from past mistakes and sometimes stumble right back into the old way of doing things. Nor do we learn from the mistakes of others. You might be one of the people whose mother and father seemed to be the dumbest people on earth for many years. At some point, however, you came to grow into the wisdom they possessed all along. Kind of like our nation right now. We're unwilling to learn from other countries' mistakes. We have to take the dive ourselves, only to find the water is cold and very shallow. Once we personally plunge into a bad choice in our lives, we can't go back and erase it. What's done is done. It's history. That's how we establish reputations.

History is the means by which we develop a stigma. It follows us around wherever we go – whether a nation or an individual. A politician's history can be his downfall. Regardless of how good a person he/she may be today, the media are sure to exploit a closet skeleton from twenty, thirty, even forty years prior. Some people are in repeat mode. They continue to commit the same egregious errors. If you have become a new creature in Christ, get out of the rut. Once you step out of the rut, when someone throws your past in your face, if you did it, own it, and move on. It's not who you are now.

4) Move On

Since you can't change an event in history, it is time to move on. If someone else offended you in some manner, forgive it, learn from it, recall it when necessary, but move on. If you brought about circumstances that resulted in bitter consequences or harm to others, seek their forgiveness, forgive yourself, and move on. Dwelling on some inequity serves only to exacerbate the situation. I could have withered away, or curled up in a corner somewhere, and stayed trapped inside a shell of a body. Had I done so, it would have totally changed the course of my life, and others'.

~~~

Marie is someone whom people find irritating to be around for longer than a thirty-minute interval. Visit her once and you're privy to her life's story. She's been an unproductive person for much of her life because she can't move on from her anger and bitterness. You can spare yourself the time and gasoline for another visit. Simply hit the instant replay button in your mind, and you'll have a storehouse of visits. Her conversation will be the same, almost verbatim. She's an elderly woman who has hung onto grievances that happened more than sixty years ago. Marie has complained bitterly and incessantly about perceptions she has of specific situations. Visiting her longer than the thirty-minute timeslot will be subjecting oneself to hearing a recount of the past an octave higher. Incredibly sad how this lady has allowed incidents from many years ago to completely immobilize her. Her heart is bitter, and it continues to show in her elderly age.

~~~

It would be easier to stay motionless in life. Just let the world go on around you. Get your education, get married, rear a family, and draw a paycheck. Sounds like a good plan. Or, you can choose to do none of the above. Either scenario is just getting by. Getting by translates into stuck. Immovable. Not advancing. Trapped in the same place you've been for years. The problem with getting by is you tend to have no purpose. Having no purpose can lean toward depression. Depression finds you in a state of despair. You suddenly become wrapped up in a meaningless world, and that can be very miserable.

A meaningless life is one that doesn't move forward. It attracts some unpleasant cellmates like confusion, anger, resentment, bitterness, hurt, and gloom. These vampires feed off of their victims. They steal your joy, contentment, peace, and your personal relationship and communion with God. Stalemate is not the answer to being set free from a prison of your past, nor anticipation of losing those fugitive garments. Our goal should be to become active, vibrant, effective and content in whatever situation we find ourselves. Whether we have a family or are living alone, we can make a difference in our world. We have avenues by which to become effective for Christ — our family, friends, work, church, and community.

~~~

Do not grieve the Holy Spirit of God, with whom you were sealed for the day of redemption. Get rid of all bitterness, rage and anger, brawling and slander, along with every form of malice. Be kind and compassionate to one another, forgiving each other, just as in Christ God forgave you.

~Ephesians 4:30-32

~~~

Our attitude will affect our effectiveness. Our attitude will "cause" our effectiveness. Our attitude will affect our effectiveness, because it likely will "shape" it, as well. We decide each day how we will begin it. Will I go through the day resentful and angry, bitter and hateful? Will I be tormented and torment those around me? Will I make the most of this day? Will I be kind and compassionate, forgiving and helpful? Will I make life for those around me easier? Will I be content in all things, whatever lot is cast for me? The second scenario even sounds inviting. Imagine what would happen if we actually put it into action.

5) Relinquish Your Fugitive Status

Now that you've learned some important principles in how to turn in that prison garb, it's time to relinquish your fugitive status. It's your choice. Is it going to be a positive decision or a poor choice you make? It's a poor choice if you stay where you are and not advance to "go." You hold the key. You've had it all along. It's found in His Word – the Holy Bible. His Word was the key to every dark cellblock in your heart. Inside those cellblocks were the hurts with different names, different faces, and different issues attached to them.

Every imaginable issue we have facing us in this 21st century, God's word covers them all! He knew before He spoke this world into existence we would need a way out of our silent prisons. He realized we would need ways and means to cope in the present, regardless of how vile our world became. That's why He sent Jesus. That's why His unimpeachable plan was documented in order to provide answers to every situation we would face today. Technology has not outdated God's database of information. The more advanced our lives become, the more encompassing His remedies for life's issues. His ancient words remain timeless tools in every culture we generate.

Allow the godly people the Lord has placed along your path to be your aides. Trying to rid oneself of past encumbrances unassisted can be difficult. It can be done, but it surely helps to have others waiting to pick up the slack for you. Imagine having a severe physical injury and trying to wait on yourself at home without an aide to assist you. It is even more comforting when that someone loves you. Likewise, having someone who cares for you deeply promotes healing from past injuries.

God often sends His wisdom through messengers. With eyes wide open, we must be willing recipients of wholesome spiritual aid. All too often I see couples who struggle because one or the other builds walls around his or her heart. The individual won't allow his/her spouse, or anyone else for that matter, to help set life back on course. It makes for a miserable family existence.

~~~

Art worked for a company for twenty-two years when the company went belly-up. He had planned to retire from the company. Not only did he lose his job, he also lost his retirement due to mismanagement of funds. Art went into a deep depression and soon distanced himself from his family. His wife and family encouraged Art to send résumés to other companies in his specialty, or to look for a different line of work. Art resented any suggestions they made. Christian friends spoke with Art, offered him jobs, all of which he rejected, including their wise counsel. He found himself in the throes of deep despair.

Art became a prisoner inside the walls he erected during his depression. He ultimately lost his house and property, and the respect of his family. Art eventually stepped out of his prison, but could not let go of the past anger. There is still tension in the family, and his wife confesses he is not the man she married. His heart is not amenable to tenderness any longer. Laughter is no longer sprinkled in their days. He has chosen to trade his joy with his children and now his grandchildren for sorrow over material possessions.

~~~

Why do we build walls? Someone we love inflicts one painful injury, and the walls go up. It's like we have this secret button we push, and out of the floors of our heart come towering walls. They were there ready to assume position at our command. But for many, there's only an up button. They never come down.

Walls have a purpose. They're erected for protection. They're designed to keep out the unwanted, the uninvited, the unwelcomed. They also serve the purpose for no one to see in. What if it's messy inside? What if my décor isn't acceptable, unworthy of viewing? Perhaps I have secrets I don't want anyone to know about. People might look differently at me if they knew my undisclosed past. If I let someone know my hurts, he/she may hurt me in the same way. Perhaps that's why my walls went up, because the hurt came back. It didn't feel good. Its sting was too familiar. It took me a long time to recover from the last blow; I can't let that happen again. I will never give that much of myself away to anyone.

Or, maybe I have a treasure I don't want to share. People protect treasures, you know. They stow them away in a safe place so those they don't trust can't touch them. What if someone stole the treasure? Perhaps someone already did once. It took a long time to find it and bring it back to its rightful place. What if I'm scared to let you see my treasure? You may not guard it as I do. You may not protect it. It's valuable. If you break it, I may never find all the pieces again. It's been broken once, and it's fragile. A mere whisper at the wrong time could cause it to crumble. I'll just hold it close, thank you. You can love me at a distance, but you can never see the riches I have stored behind the walls of my heart.

~~~

"I'm so glad, Lord, I opened my heart to You. By opening it to Your richness, I allowed blessings to be poured in and spilled out in great abundance. Your plan was more perfect than any I could have devised for myself. Your love for me is glorious!"
                                                                                    Amen.

~~~

Don't be afraid to relinquish your fugitive status. You have the tools to equip you to strip those garments once and for all, so get rid of the evidence. As you develop a deeper dependency on God, your anxiety will begin to dissipate. People will hurt you again, but your contentment in those times of heartache will measure differently from before. You're preparing for fullness in your life.

That's what being liberated is all about — learning to move about freely in the richness of love, trust, and faith in God to walk through your journey of life without fear of what ruins lay behind you.

6) Give Time Time

I'm an impatient person by nature. It accompanies the mover-and-shaker personality God equipped me with. I enjoy productivity. I also enjoy getting things accomplished on the topside of life rather than sliding into procrastination. As my agenda increases, so does the demand for my time. Consequently, it appears as though I have dragged my feet and put off the inevitable, when truly that isn't the case at all.

My fast-paced life coincides with my accelerated strides. However, I think I travel fast until my husband and I go for a walk. His gait-speed exceeds mine by almost a full step. It's not a problem initially, but by the time we have walked 50 yards, the distance between us increases. I don't mind it during a casual walk as much as I do when we're shopping together, and especially when I'm in my heels. *There's method to his madness. Walking briskly leaves little time for window-shopping, and less time for temptation. Smart man. (I wonder if he's ever known I was onto him all this time!)* There are times I want, and even need, him by my side as opposed to running off ahead of me. I'm quick to kick it up a notch and catch up, or I gently pull his hand and he knows to slow it down to accommodate my pace. It's amazing the two of us have enjoyed a blissful marriage. We mirror in strong leadership qualities, yet have learned to balance our attributes to complement one another as opposed to make it a struggle. *And they say opposites attract. Hhm. What do they know?*

Impatience has gotten me ahead of God more times than I care to share. God has all the time in eternity. He doesn't get in a big hurry over much of anything. He doesn't rush through decisions. In fact, He encourages us to pray without ceasing. Now, I don't mean to suggest to you that God needs time to weigh in on all the evidence in order to decide how things will play out. After all,

His omniscience negates that school of thought. I am suggesting, however, that He allows sufficient time for hearts and wills to change in order for His perfect plan for our lives to be revealed and enjoyed.

~~~

I often wonder had I grown impatient in my suffering at home and succumbed to the offer to elope with my high school honey, how different my life would have been. Would I have remained in the same town? Had that occurred, my past would have been staring me in the face day in and day out. Moving away from the people who had brought me physical and emotional harm, as well as from those who chose to ignore my plea for help, was part of a greater plan than just my restoration. Every move Webby and I have made in our covenant relationship/ministry was part of bringing us to a service that needed our touch to accomplish what God had equipped us to do for His people.

Yes, there always are mistakes along the way. Unwise decisions on our part and others' roles as well, including unfaithfulness from church members and friends. It accompanies daily living. Disagreements are a part of being people. What those times bring us should be a closer dependency upon God. The troublesome times are when we should fall on our face before God, surrender to His healing power, and allow Him to guide us safely out of the storm we've gotten caught in. It is an opportunity to trust God explicitly with the details of situations, even and especially when everything blows up in our face.

None of us escape those trials in life. We shouldn't want to, really. I know that's hard to wrap your head around, initially. But when you think about it, we grow best and strongest through times of extreme adversity. While hardships are painful, they are opportunities for us to become more intimately connected with the Lord of our lives. He longs for that. Oh, not for you to go through trials, so much as He longs for your dependence upon Him.

Look at adversity as an opportunity to get back in step with God. He paces all His steps, and when you're following alongside God, or even a step behind Him, your steps are more deliberate, as well.

~~~

Remember to give time time. Be patient with God and those who love you. Don't expect things to happen overnight. Pray without ceasing, expecting a radical release. It may take years before God breaks you free from a difficult situation. That's not a comforting thought – years. When you're in the midst of a severe trial, you can get physically worn out from the spiritual warfare, let alone the emotional drain it brings.

~~~

Penny was young and vibrant. She fell in love and married before finishing college. Her husband, ten years older, was divorced and had two children by his first wife. She and George were strong believers. They both were fortunate to grow up in God-fearing homes. They were blessed with one child before George incurred a severe on-the-job injury leaving him physically and partially mentally impaired. He remains disabled to this day. Penny's life has been challenged with caring for George in the home while being the main financial provider for the family, as well as encumbered with all family responsibilities.

Penny watched the hands of time as the years clicked off her youth. Their child is now grown with a family. George's children ceased being involved in their dad's life years ago. The burden continues to take a physical toll on Penny. She is exhausted from the strenuous, rigorous, mundane lifestyle.

Penny has remained steadfast under extreme adversity, not always happy in her silent prison, but keeping her trust and faith in God. Temptations have come; she has resisted her will to give in. Penny has a buttressed commitment to her covenant relationship. It would have been much easier for her to have placed George in a facility and have him cared for by trained professionals. Instead, Penny has been his primary caregiver, touching George's tormented body with the same loving hands he was accustomed to before his accident.

Time has stood still for Penny all these years. The reward of her dedication is best recognized in the hearts of George and Penny for now. But great it will be when she meets her Lord and He says, "Well done, thy good and faithful servant."

~~~

I didn't marry the young man I'd dated forever, as easy as that might have been for temporary escape. He was a great guy. He respected me. He and I had shared four years together. But, being my husband wasn't his part in God's plan for my life. I had no idea he would be my ticket to the heart God had prepared for me – the answer to my six-year prayer!

153

I could have been like my siblings and decided to live the only way we had been taught. Most of my brothers would engage in multiple marriages, abuse, alcohol, drugs and brokenness. My sister would marry a man who abused her for fifteen years. I was the only child out of eight in our family who broke the chain of dysfunction. I acted on free will, but so did they. We each had the opportunity to pick up the cross rather than the pitchfork, if you will, and move on to something greater in our lives.

Why was I spared? Was I the fair-haired child? Was I "God's chosen one?" Emphatically, no! He doesn't love me any more or less than He loves them. The challenge to step outside of "familiar" was equally available to each one of my family members.

I chose to trust God with my life. Yes, I fell in love with a godly man, but I chose to trust God in that decision. I decided to move on. I determined to become effective in my life for Christ. I settled on living for God. I wouldn't do it all right all the time. I've had my share of blunders along the way. It would take me years to grow into the fullness of the Lord, and He's still not finished with me. I am still a lot of work in progress. I fall short of His will for my life, confess, repent, and move on daily. I make that choice anew each day.

My siblings would catch up to the Lord later on, and I am thankful they have drawn closer to Him. I spent much time in prayer for each of them. I love them. They are part of my heritage — the bad and good memories. My family helped shape my life, and we share good relationships with one another today. God is healing. His grace is sufficient for all things. He paves the way when we walk alongside or behind Him. Getting ahead of God's perfect timing can find us tripping on our own sequence of events.

Impatience can be a stumbling block in adverse situations. Wait on God's answer for your way out. It may take years to get out of the pickle you're in, but trusting God to help you clearly define your path for exiting will keep you from making a bigger mess of things. He is infinitely wise in counsel. He knows your situations inside and out, up and down, everything that has happened in the past, what is going on presently, and the future of every detail of your life. That should afford you a great amount of comfort when trusting Him with your adversities and giving Him all the time He needs to accomplish His best for your life. Just give time time and wait on God's perfect timing.

~~~

> Oh, the depth of the riches of the wisdom and knowledge of God!
>
> How unsearchable his judgments, and his paths beyond tracing out!
>
> "Who has known the mind of the Lord? Or who has been his counselor?"
>
> "Who has ever given to God, that God should repay them?"
>
> For from him and through him and for him are all things.
>
> To him be the glory forever! Amen.   ~Romans 11:33-36 (NIV)

7) A Jail-Break

Some of us are more vulnerable to stay shackled to the past than others and then to keep looking over our shoulders once we've stepped out of prison. We like staying in our "comfortable prison garb." It doesn't look so pretty on us, but we've kind of learned to "relax" in the attire. It's easier to stay in a familiar setting, even if it's an unhealthy one, rather than explore how to shed ourselves completely of the past once we've made a jail-break.

If you're without the power of the Holy Spirit, fighting becomes a battle you won't win. You're fighting against forces much greater than yourself. On the other hand, when you team up with God, fighting for freedom becomes something rewarding. You get results. You feel empowered. You begin to experience changes within you that are clearly God's reshaping of your life. Oh, sure, there are going to be days where you can't pull yourself out of the bleakness. It's human nature. But these days will become fewer and farther between. Be patient with the Lord, and yourself.

By the time my prayer was being answered, I was a living testimony of how God could transform a little girl – broken, abused, and destitute – hear her prayer, and then use her to bring a message about His redemption and grace. Yes, God busted me; He set me free. It was jail-break for me by the hands of the Almighty King who reigns supreme, not only in my life, but among the principalities of this world! He had busted "me" out of jail! Then, the question became: How do I shuck the exposed evidence that I was a jailbird once upon a time?

Working on a farm and performing chores around home gives a gal a lot of time to ponder. Many times my thoughts would find me working through injurious heartache, trying to weigh it against God's teachings at my undercover Bible time. The rhythmic sweep of the broom launched me into mesmeric thought patterns. Each swipe seemed to promote bullet-point strategies for me to get through one more day. I would attempt to pick a letter from the alphabet, and then choose words to fit my specific need(s). *Easier to remember; for me, at least. I'm kind of fond of simplicity. Why complicate life any more than it already is, eh?* As I slipped into my new life, I would apply the same scriptures I had trusted before, but today – the new present – from a different perspective. I didn't want to appear free; I wanted to be free. So, if sweeping meant thinking, then best I roll up my sleeves and get to work.

God's provision plan for my life came. Many times I was unaware that He had dropped in for confirmation until the evidence hit me square between the eyes. The specific points I prayed for would come. Not all at once. Not even in the order in which I had prayed for them. And often, I didn't even recognize them until much later in my life. As I said earlier, it is a process, and I had to give time time.

~~~

But you, brothers and sisters, are not in darkness so that this day should surprise you like a thief. You are all children of the light and children of the day. We do not belong to the night or to the darkness. So then, let us not be like others, who are asleep, but let us be awake and sober. For those who sleep, Sleep at night, and those who get drunk, get drunk at night. But since we belong to the day, let us be sober, putting on faith and love as a breastplate, and the hope of salvation as a helmet. For God did not appoint us to suffer wrath but to receive salvation through our Lord Jesus Christ. He died for us so that, whether we are awake or asleep, we may live together with him. Therefore encourage one another and build each other up, just as in fact you are doing. Now we ask you, brothers and sisters, to acknowledge those who work hard among you, who care for you in the Lord and who admonish you. Hold them in the highest regard in love because of their work.

Live in peace with each other. And we urge you, brothers and sisters, warn those who are idle and disruptive, encourage the disheartened, help the weak, be patient with everyone. Make sure that nobody pays back wrong for wrong, but always strive to do what is good for each other and for everyone else.

Rejoice always, pray continually, give thanks in all circumstances; for this is God's will for you in Christ Jesus.

~I Thessalonians 5:4-18 (NIV)

~ ~ ~

These bullet-point provisions I learned in my walk with God are suitable for any past, present or future adversity you may want to overcome. They are simple, but demand patience. I continue to benefit from these blessings today.

- **Presence** – "Lord, grace me with Your Holy presence every day. Should I step out of Your light, blind me with Your company. Weigh me down with Your companionship."

- **Praise** – "Let me never forget to praise You, Lord. There are no other gods like You. I have blessings I do not deserve. Thank You for Your power and majesty, and for being the King in my life."

- **Promise** – "Reveal to me your promises, God. I love knowing You have something better in store for me."

- **Patience** – "Be patient with me as I learn about You. And then, teach me why I must be patient. I know You say I need to be, but please show me that it pays to be. Please give me sufficient patience with less frustration."

- **Peace** – "Grant me inner peace, Dear God. Don't let anxiety rob me of what is rightfully mine through You."

157

- **Protection** – "Defend me, Father, when Satan tries to snare me. I don't want to be enslaved to the person I no longer am. Guard me from my enemies. You have protected me all this time. Continue to show Your mercies and favor on me."

- **Plan** – "Equip me to carry out whatever plan You have in store for me. I don't want to disappoint You, Lord."

- **Plant** – "Keep my feet planted on the path of righteousness. Impair me should I wander too far from Your way."

- **Prepare** – "May I be prepared for days to come. Teach me discernment and make me wise to the intentions of people."

- **Purpose** – "Show me Your purpose for my life. And when you do, may I be able to accomplish every task You have for me. And, God, may it always be pleasing to You."

- **Provision** – "I rejoice that I am a child of the King! Thank You for the provisions You have made for me, and those to come. May I never cease to be grateful for all You have provided."

~~~

We don't always know God's purpose for the trials in our lives. We can't even attribute Him with their origin. Many times trials in our lives are brought about by our own doing, or at the hands of someone else. But, what we can be assured of is that God will use each adversity we face for the good of those who love Him. We are also assured we don't go through them without His presence. We may not acknowledge it, recognize it, or tap into it, but He is an ever-present God. If we but ask, He will provide the guidance and truth for every situation, which eventually becomes our past.

~~~

I met Webby in the fall of 1970. We had our first date in 1971, and were married in the same year. The day we got married, my dad would go on a tirade, because the last thing he wanted me to do was to get married — especially to an out-of-town boy. That meant I would leave home, and his control! On the day that should have been a joyful occasion — my wedding day, I faced my biggest and fiercest battle with Dad. The argument over my getting married resulted in fisticuffs. I was bound and determined he would not blacken my eyes or disfigure my face on my wedding day, and I dug in my heels. God gave me the strength to hold my own that morning. When the smoke settled, I had broken broom and mop handles over Dad's head and conked him a good one on his noggin' with a lamp. I had suffered some bruises, but not visible with the long-sleeved wedding gown on. I grabbed my keys, my meager belongings and exited. It was a more abrupt exit than I had planned for my departure from home, but I wasted no time. I spent the entire day in seclusion at the minister's house, waiting to be claimed by my bridegroom that night at 8:00.

I emerged from my isolation to find my dad in his truck outside the church. Who knows how long he had waited. I wanted no scene at the church. I boldly marched over to his truck to demand him to leave. Through tear-filled eyes, he offered what is probably the only apology he's ever uttered to this day. For whatever reason, I agreed to have him escort me down the aisle. The picture captured by the photographer of me being escorted on his arm captures a thousand stories. His face is filled with shame and regret. Mine is focused only on Webby, as I was on a journey to step out of my childhood prison into the hope of better days ahead.

~ ~ ~

How I walked out of my past, and when, was a choice I would have to make. I could have remained hostage to the trials it presented, or I could allow God to be a party to my jail-break. Actually, it was jail-break twice for this gal — once would be from my home life, which created the prison in my mind; the other would be God busting me out of my fugitive status. How special I am to Him.

Continue working through your past. Be patient and wait on God to supply the provisions you specifically request. He'll keep breaking you free from your past until you shed every bit of evidence that you had that was debilitating. God will, that is, as long as you allow Him to work in your life. You are that special to Him, too.

8) Surviving the Past Means Turning It Over to God

Why would people decide to break away from a bad situation – a situation that has kept them beaten down, fearful, depressed, stressed, downtrodden – and then hang onto it for the rest of their lives? There are countless people doing just that today! They simply will not relinquish what they say they have turned over to God. Today: "Here you go, Lord." Next day: "Oops, need it back today, Lord. Thanks for watching it for me, but I'll take over from here." And, off they go ... dragging it around again.

When you walk away, leave it behind you. If you're ever going to survive the past, don't look back. If you see the red exit sign, take it. So what if it's the stairs instead of the elevator. Take the stairs! He has paved the way for your escape. Don't hesitate. Anticipate His answer to your prayer. Six years sounds like a long time to wait. Some people wait twenty or thirty years before they ever see God's plan come together fully.

Christians anticipate the return of Jesus. We simply don't know when it will be. Nonetheless, we must be ready to exit when He comes. There'll be no time for correction once He's here. That decision must be made ahead of time. It will happen in the blink of an eye, and He will fulfill a promise from thousands of years ago. It is God's call, not ours, when that day shall come to pass. We are only called to be prepared.

God alone can set us free from ourselves. He alone can set us on a course that releases us from a past that haunts us. Your past is a part of who you are, but not who you are now. Don't be bitter, or angry, or resentful about having been there. Never use it as a crutch or allow it to drag you down, but praise God for bringing you through it. Count everything you've gone through a victory, whether it's a past from yesterday or forty years ago. Present your complaint to Him, for someone does care for you. He has brought you this far. Continue searching for godly wisdom. What you have become is because of who you were. You can't change it. It's time to move into the present and never look back.

~~~

I cry aloud to the Lord; I lift up my voice to the Lord for mercy. I pour out my complaint before him; before him I tell my trouble. When my spirit grows faint within me, it is you who know my way. In the path where I walk, men have hidden a snare for me. Look to my right and see; no one is concerned for me. I have no refuge; no one cares for my life. I cry to you, O Lord; I say, "You are my refuge, my portion in the land of the living." Listen to my cry, for I am in desperate need; rescue me from those who pursue me, for they are too strong for me. Set me free from my prison, that I may praise your name. Then the righteous will gather about me because of your goodness to me.

~Psalm 142

~~~

> *The chain of guilt is a strong one. It is also one that gives no wriggle room.*

21

Part 2: Fugitive in the Present

From Past to Path

Let's fast-forward to 1983. Webby and I will have been married almost twelve years. I had been serving *and* growing in the Lord during this period of time. Through the grace of God, the prayer I had uttered – "Lord, please send someone to teach me how to love" had continued to multiply. I experienced variety in love every day. God had handpicked a great man for me. Webby had surrendered his life to Christ a few years before we met. What I was growing to respect more about him was that he not only put on the cloak of Christ, he lived out Christ in his life. He was completely committed to God, and truly adopted the attitude of "loving your wife as Christ loves the Church."

Now, I don't mean to infer that every day was a bed of roses, because truly it was not. Comparatively speaking, when I measured it to the homelife I grew up in, it was pretty near great, even at its worst! I have the utmost faith in God's magnificent wisdom. God knew when He patched up my husband's heart that He would need to stitch in an extra measure of patience so that Webby could deal with me. I believe that's why Webby is so tender to and for me. *Ah, forget the fact that Webby is like that with everybody. I like to claim that as my exclusive gift.*

What would impress me most in my private life – a life I had not by then totally shared with my husband, and to a great extent still have not – I was very pleased that I *allowed* my husband to love me. I didn't block his attempts to teach me how to love, nor my desire to return it. I was so hungry for love that there would be no denial of the passage to my heart, or the reciprocation of my love to him. It didn't happen just by chance. I would pray day after day, silently to myself, during the times when we were intimate with each other, number one, that God would empower me to be open, to trust, to welcome, to receive the love Webby would share with me. Secondly, that I would be able to express it and give it back abundantly – even more than he loved me. *Which was going to be a lot!*

I would be plowing through God's Word to tenderize my heart and to free up this guilty feeling that kept tugging at my soul. The guilt would creep into my mind and even the tiniest crevices of my heart. It would render me a long-distance slave, if you will, to my family and all that I endured and suffered.

I had reconciled with God in sharing no part in the occurrences at home. My guilt focused on knowing my mother and younger siblings, especially my sister, continued to suffer through the hell, while I had been released. I felt guilty for escaping and was invoking a sentence upon myself for leaving them there. And so, I would suffer with them. How could I think of what they were going through without a full understanding of the pain? I knew what it felt like. I understood what they were facing. And I wasn't there to help. These thoughts would rob me of my sleep, rest, comfort, peace, joy, and my communion with the Lord. I didn't realize how much I was giving up by allowing the memories to take over so much of my inner self.

I couldn't explain it to anyone; not even, and especially, Webby. It was very much my personal, private secret at that point … still, after all those years! I was confident I would be less accepted and less loved if anyone knew my full background. Dismissing this darkness in my past was actually very healthy, and healing, but it wasn't the cure. It was just putting the past in remission, kind of like cancer.

~~~

I have a young friend — he's single; in his late twenties. The day of his twenty-first birthday, Billy was diagnosed with leukemia and wasn't supposed to make it. He was in college in Florida; his parents in Indiana. He would inhabit a room at Good Samaritan Hospital in West Palm Beach for a year under the care of an excellent oncologist. I got involved with Billy through his mom, a receptionist at one of the law firms of a client of mine.

I sponsored a team for a golf benefit at the PGA in West Palm where Billy worked at the time. He had aspirations, and all the ingredients, to become a golf pro. That life was permanently put on hold for Billy. My "Move A Mountain Prayer Ministry," along with Billy's parents' church and multitudes of others began praying for Billy and his family. Through God's intervention and the assistance of a great team of medical professionals, Billy defied the odds. In fact, Billy got the green light on his five-year remission marker. That's the big one, you know — you make it five years, they really feel it's a milestone.

I continue to pray for Billy to this very day. God has a great purpose for him. Part of my prayer is that Billy will unveil and fulfill his mission.

If you know anyone who's had cancer, you understand how the remission thing works. You constantly have to be reminded of what you went through, because it could come back when you least expect it. You go through a battery of bloodwork to test your markers, and then hold your breath and do an awful lot of praying that the results will come back negative.

Cancer is a nasty past that haunts its victim and the families forever. Pray for the children who contract it. Pray for the adults, as well. Pray for a cure. Pray that God will "kill the beast!"

~~~

Isn't that a picture of our past? It's like a cancer. We make that one-year, two-year, perhaps even make it to the five-year milestone; we think it's in full remission, and all of a sudden, it's meeting us around the bend again. Why? What triggers the instant-replay button in our heads? It can be so frustrating, and really cause you to question if your faith is in place.

All these thoughts are like little atoms swirling in your head! Flowing, buzzing, flying, flitting; it's a wonder they don't collide. Maybe that's why we have nightmares, because they actually do! The instant-replay button has a magnet in it and it's labeled – "bad memories." And once a bad memory gets in close proximity, *WHAM!* It draws in its magnetic field, and it comes at such force that it activates the replay button, and once it does, you're in for a fitful day or night!

As I stated earlier, I've never been to a counselor. I have nothing against them, mind you. I have some great friends who are the best of counselors. Counselors serve a great purpose, and many of them do their job very well. *I prefer Christian over the non, however.* But, digging up bones has never been my method of resolution. I knew I wanted no part of that. But sometimes, it doesn't take sitting and pondering to bring them up. I tend to think that same complex mind that traps all the memories and swirls them around also has a protective mechanism. It can block some bad memories. Some say that's healthy; most say it's not.

I'm glad my mind blocked some. I know it did, because I catch glimpses, but I don't want to sit and ponder about them. I don't want to give Satan that kind of time out of my life, nor that kind of power! Why would I want to recall the vivid facts? Don't need to, thank you.

~~~

I was watching the movie "Schindler's List" – remember that one? – and the Germans were flushing out the Jews from their homes. There's a scene where they burst into a room, as I recall a motel room or an apartment bedroom, and there was a bed. I remember them opening fire on the mattress. And suddenly someone fell. He had been hanging onto the slats of the frame. That was a triggering event for a terrible memory of mine.

Perhaps I didn't mind, after all, sitting up with my mom till the wee hours of the morning putting up those vegetables. I always hoped that my perpetrators would be fast asleep so that I could. That was not always the case. So, I would hide. In the closet. In a corner. Under the bed. But there were times that I hung onto the slats of the frame underneath the bed. It worked a few times, but I had long hair, and on a moonlit night, I got grabbed by the head of the hair and yanked out from underneath. Consequently, I remember little else from the movie at that point.

So, I have enough memories. Don't need more. Why dig them up? It works for some people. For me, it's not the appropriate approach. Don't want to know any more than I do already. Don't want to give Satan that part of my mind! It's mine, and he can't have it!

~~~

The Naked Truth

I had studied God's Word. I knew what I must do. I had to forgive, and I can tell you, I had done that. At least the exercise in my head and heart was completed. What I had not done was to forgive my oppressors face to face. And *that*, my dear, was probably not going to happen. And that was that. I was fine with the idea. I was coping with the pasts. No one had ever known the ins and outs of what I had endured; those details had been between God and me, and that's where they would stay.

You can't visit God's Word and misunderstand His instruction about forgiveness. You can ignore it, but you can't misconstrue it. It's the naked truth about His redemption. I was well aware of what the Word said and would be reminded again and again what I needed to do. The Gospel of Matthew deals with this very issue.

And again, I'd say, "Lord, don't ask me to do that. I can deal with this. I'm doing just fine. Don't ask me again, please. I'm not strong enough. I don't know how. I simply can't. I just won't." And so, I remained an escapee. Not in prison, just a fugitive. I would balk at the Lord's will for me in this important link to liberty. Praising Him and feeling blessed about my release from prison. But, the urging by the Holy Spirit I would keep at bay for now.

The Lord was unrelenting. He would pursue me because He loves me that much. I had prayed a prayer; He had not forgotten. It had fallen on His ears, and once it landed there, He was all over it. *Be careful what you pray for, because you might just get it!*

God knew if I were to be completely redeemed, I would need to follow His steps to redemption. I couldn't just pick and choose my path. It was a well mapped-out direction. Failing to accept the key and step through another door would be like setting sail for a South Seas vacation but forgetting to climb aboard the yacht!

It was clear God had a different plan for me. I would resist until God was done with that part of my stubborn will. He would soon use an opportunity that would cause me not only to open the last prison door, but also to shed my prison garb once and for all. God would send a messenger to tell me, "Honey, your stripes are showing." My past would soon take a different path.

22

Part 2: Fugitive in the Present

Key of Hope

Back to 1983. Webby and I were serving at a large Christian church in the Atlanta, Georgia area. Actually, that was our first full-time ministry. We'd been there since '77 – me as a church secretary initially; Webby joining the following year – and we served there for eighteen years. *They didn't want us to leave. We've only been in two full-time ministries. We feel very blessed.* We were lying in bed one night, just yakking about our day. Webby began telling me about a problem with one of the youth in the church he had learned of that day. A beautiful teenage girl had come in to talk to one of the ministers. She began to pour out her heart about being molested at home. Webby had been called into the meeting, and the two guys were pretty torn up over the whole ordeal and quite uncertain about the validity of the story.

Webby continued, terribly distraught as he was relating the story. He rambled on. My thoughts were elsewhere. I knew immediately God's perfect timing was in play. Webby continued, "We just don't know whether to believe her or not. You know this family. They're as good as they come. Now, does she seem to you to be a likely candidate for molestation?"

My heart was dying for this young girl, and for her family. But, you know what? It happens to the best of families. Unfortunately, many times, no one believes the victim. There it was – the moment of truth. It had fallen on my shoulders to be the advocate for this precious girl. I took a deep breath before responding to his question.

"Do I?" There was a silence that ripped through the darkness and a chilled stillness scalded to the bone. I felt Webby go limp beside me. He honestly had never suspected anything to that extent. He knew about the physical and verbal abuse, but had never suspicioned the sexual. It was a mixed-feeling moment. Did I revel in the fact that I was able to disguise the shameful acts for seventeen years, or did I recoil for fear it would turn our fairytale marriage into shambles?

The thought had not so much as rolled off my brow as he wrapped me up in his loving, protective arms. He wept over me and with me and told me how sorry he was, that I didn't deserve it. It was a moment that God had *known* would happen. He knew it at the time I was being abused years before. God in His all-knowing, all-caring, all-healing power had prepared my husband for such a time as this. God knew Webby would partner-up with me in getting me past the past. Now you, too, understand why God saved this man's heart for me.

~~~

God would use the unveiling of my long suppressed secret to work in this young girl's life. Webby would report to the minister involved with a newfound conviction about who fit the mold of potential victims of sexual abuse. The matter was reported and handled through the senior minister at the church from that point, but the young lady's voice was heard.

This was definitely a turning point for me, an awakening of sorts. It was becoming apparent that God planned to use my experience in order to organize a jail-break for others.

This was the first step, but a huge one in that it was the first time I had shared that part of my history with anyone. That secret was something only God and I shared, and, of course, my perpetrators. I suspected this was the case with the young girl, as well.

It takes a tremendous amount of courage to entrust your image to someone. The fear is the person you tell will judge you as the one at fault. Many have been falsely judged. The sentence is a life of being someone who has "stability" issues and one is marked with the label of "beware." It is a risk to talk.

~~~

Next Key, Please

It's funny, because all along God kept telling me throughout His Word, assuring me in my prayer life, soothing my heart and calming my fears that everything would be all right. I just wouldn't listen to Him. It wasn't a voice that I heard in my ear. It was a flood of peace that kept sweeping over me day after day, week after week, year after year. And it was that same sweet peace I had known at the mantel prayer that day. My will – that stubborn human will kept resisting it! I didn't want to go back to face my enemy, because I feared it would be like going back to prison. Rather, it was the key that would "almost" let me step out of that fugitive status once and for all.

But, God was not through with the process yet. No, there would be more. I could have been content to remain in that safe place – Webby's arms. Had I done so, I would have missed other blessings and not have fulfilled God's purpose in my life.

The key God handed to me that day through Webby was the last "key of hope" to release me from bondage. The next key to be handed me would be the "key of faith." It would eventually guide me to the "key of peace." I had resisted this one key for years. Now, my secret was no longer hidden. My cover was blown and my stripes were exposed. The one person's affection that I didn't want to compromise finally knew ... the rest of my story.

~~~

> Guide me in your truth and teach me, for you are God my Savior, and my hope is in you all day long.
>
> ~Psalm 25:5

23

Part 2: Fugitive in the Present

Key of Faith

Luke's account of "The Cost of Following Jesus" is an insightful expression of how our effectiveness for God is thwarted by our looking back at the past instead of the past looking on at us.

In Luke 9:57-62, the author tells us, "As they were walking along the road, a man said to him, 'I will follow you wherever you go.' Jesus replied. 'Foxes have holes and birds of the air have nests, but the Son of Man has no place to lay his head.'" *Hmm, do you really want to come along?*

"Jesus said to another man, 'Follow me.' But the man replied, 'Lord, first let me go and bury my father.' Jesus said to him,

'Let the dead bury their own dead, but you go and proclaim the kingdom of God.'" *Could I do that? Could you?*

"Still another said, 'I will follow you, Lord; but first let me go back and say good-bye to my family.' Jesus replied, 'No one who puts his hands to the plow and looks back is fit for service in the kingdom of God.'" *Yikes, this got my attention!*

As a young girl, I plowed fields. It was by tractor – thank goodness! But, when you plow a garden or a tobacco row, you have to pick out an object ahead of you, line it up with your tires, and stay on course. I remember learning the hard way about that trick. Even though I had been told, I couldn't stand it. I had to look back to make sure my rows were straight. They were. Initially. The next time I'd look back, I'd see the crook in the row where I had gotten off course looking back the first time. Glancing back again, there'd be a second crook. Again, a third. My rows would end up looking like a snake. I was embarrassed, my brothers would laugh at me, and my dad would get upset. You see, once the plants are growing, you have to follow those crooks in the row in order to fertilize, spray for insects, and then to harvest. It hampered the whole process.

Jesus said it Himself: no one – that means you and me – is fit for service if he looks back. I don't care how adept we think we are, how well we think we can manage focusing in both directions, Jesus doesn't think we're fit for service in His Kingdom if we keep glancing back at the injustices, mistakes and misguided steps of our past. In fact, He was so adamant that He didn't even make an allowance for these guys going back to tell their families good-bye, nor to wait to bury their dead. Don't misconstrue the intent of his message. It doesn't mean you're not welcome in His Kingdom; He just doesn't believe you're going to be as effective for convincing others about the Good News of His name. He needs those of us who are focused on looking forward, who pick out a target and keep to the course, not revisiting old habits, our sordid past, or allowing those things to hamper our testimony. He desires for us to stay focused on the things about His business rather than mulling over past experiences that get us bogged down and/or distracted in our service.

God's Got Your Back

> Where I am afraid, I will put my trust in Thee.
>
> ~Psalm 56:3

~~~

Faith is a stronghold for us. It is our anchor. The psalmist trusted in his faith of the Almighty's protection. In the face of fear, he relied on his faith to trust God with the plan for his days. He didn't lose heart, even though his enemy continued to press down. He held fast to the God who loved him sufficiently at all times, even when he was unlovely. God had his back; he didn't need to look back to see who might be coming.

Having faith in a tomorrow that seems never to come can be an overwhelming thought when you're caught in adversity. But, holding on to find an avenue that will lead you out of despair requires faith. Making sure your faith is grounded in the only One who can cover you, protect you, and lead you safely out of your storm is the difference in knowing a peace that passes all understanding and living in a constant cloud of confusion. Thinking of life's troubles in terms of temporary woe, regardless of how long you've been there, can keep you from getting bogged in today's despair.

~~~

> Therefore, we do not lose heart.
>
> Though outwardly we are wasting away,
>
> Yet inwardly we are being renewed day by day.
>
> For our light and momentary troubles are
>
> Achieving for us an eternal glory that far outweighs them all.
>
> So we fix our eyes not on what is seen, but on what is unseen.
>
> For what is seen is temporary, but what is unseen is eternal.
>
> ~2 Corinthians 4:16-18 (NIV)

~~~

It's important for us to keep the faith. It is imperative that we continue to trust Him. Onward, Christian soldiers! This is our purpose in life. What possible good can be accomplished for God or you in looking back, regretting what was, wishing for things that can never be, and holding on to the hate, anger and bitterness that spoils the beauty of today? God's perfect plan for each of us is to embrace faith in its fullness. To keep one eye on bygone days is to lose clear vision for things ahead.

The key to hope was a given. Hope is something we clamor for. No one seems to have difficulty with hoping, dreaming, and wishing for a better life. It's the key to faith that presents the difficulty. How much faith do you need to catch a glimmer of things you hope for?

~~~

He [Jesus] replied, "Because you have so little faith. I tell you the truth, if you have faith as small as a mustard seed, you can say to this mountain, 'Move from here to there' and it will move. Nothing will be impossible for you."

~Matthew 17:20-21 (NIV)

~~~

Once I learned the power I could access through prayer, my faith deepened. Once my faith deepened, my trust broadened. Once my trust broadened, I quickly learned there is nothing my God can't do.

We're Not the First

Millions have gone before us with their own key to faith. We are not the first, nor will we be the last, to need and experience God's miraculous undoing of past trauma. Others have unlocked mysteries of God's power and love and have witnessed mighty works at His hands. The impossible undoings of error in history have been made whole and perfect at His command. Tapping into God's power is only a belief away. At least, it was for me. Had I failed to pick up that key of faith and walk through other doors, I would still be exposing my stripes. *Yikes! That's a gruesome thought.*

The key of faith is at your fingertips today. It is the one key no one can pass off to you. God makes it available, but the decision is yours. You must choose to pick up the key and unlock the door to your faith. You have longed for the relationship with your Heavenly Father since your birth. Your faith in Truth will set you free. Getting past your past depends on your key to faith.

~~~

Now faith is being sure of what we hope for and certain of what we do not see. This is what the ancients were commended for.

~Hebrews 11:1-2

> *Don't sit on your will.*
> *Exercise it.*

24

Part 2: Fugitive in the Present

Coming Clean

After I had told Webby only that I had gone through some really bad times as a child, it's amazing how God began to work on setting me completely free. *I did not share the sordid details. It wasn't necessary. He didn't need to know those. (Why would I want to belabor him with that and risk having him dwell on conjured-up images in his mind?)* I hadn't heard from my father for years. Didn't take my kids around my family, quite honestly. When I visited my mom and sister, it would be one on one, or it would be a drop-in visit when my brothers and father weren't around. If she ever knew why I planned it that way, she never let on, but it was always contrived on my part. All in all, I maintained very limited contact with my dad.

Out of the blue at two o'clock one morning, our phone rings. It's my father. He's ranting and raving, on another one of his drunken binges. He's screaming into the phone, telling me how much he hates me, hates Webby, and he's going to come up to Atlanta from South Georgia and burn down our house one night while we're all asleep. As you can well imagine, that didn't go over well with me, and instead of having the good sense to hang up, I commenced to give him a piece of my mind. I didn't get many words out of my mouth when the phone was grabbed from my hands.

For the first time in my life, I didn't have to fight the battle with my dad. Webby stood in my gap, and in Christian love and with fierce diplomacy, he sobered up my father's thinking in a hairy heartbeat.

How empowering that was for me – to have my husband step in and wrestle the demon I had battled privately for all those years. But, this was a new day. I had advanced to the present now. I had emerged, progressed to a new phase in my Christian walk. And, it was the first time I really had appreciated that blessing to its fullest measure. I recall returning to sleep, praising my God for revealing how good He was to me, and for sending me my warrior here on Earth. Because I had shared my experience with my husband, he now was my partner in battle. What a newfound security I had discovered.

~~~

Together they will be like warriors in battle trampling their enemy into the mud of the streets. They will fight because the Lord is with them, and they will put the enemy horsemen to shame.

~Zechariah 10:5 (NIV)

~~~

Putting Faith into Action

The next day I began revisiting the scriptures about forgiveness – and especially Matthew 18. It would be within hours that I would hear one message of a multi-part series by Dr. Charles Stanley about forgiveness. I ordered the series on tape, and as soon as it was in hand, I told Webby I needed to go away for the weekend to fast and pray. He was a great encouragement. He took care of the kids, and he was in prayer for me as I set about my journey. I knew I had to figure out a way to rid myself of the guilt I was feeling once and for all, and when I came back, I would have the answer. It was time to put my faith into action.

~~~

... "If anyone causes one of these little ones—those who believe in me—to stumble, it would be better for them to have a large millstone hung around their neck and to be drowned in the depths of the sea. Woe to the world because of the things that cause people to stumble! Such things must come, but woe to the person through whom they come! If your hand or your foot causes you to stumble, cut it off and throw it away. It is better for you to enter life maimed or crippled than to have two hands or two feet and be thrown into eternal fire. And if your eye causes you to stumble, gouge it out and throw it away. It is better for you to enter life with one eye than to have two eyes and be thrown into the fire of hell. ...

"See that you do not despise one of these little ones. For I tell you that their angels in heaven always see the face of my Father in heaven....

"If your brother or sister sins, go and point out their fault, just between the two of you. If they listen to you, you have won them over. But if they will not listen, take one or two others along, so that 'every matter may be established by the testimony of two or three witnesses.' If they still refuse to listen, tell it to the church; and if they refuse to listen even to the church, treat them as you would a pagan or a tax collector.

"Truly I tell you, whatever you bind on earth will be bound in heaven, and whatever you loose on earth will be loosed in heaven.

"Again, truly I tell you that if two of you on earth agree about anything they ask for, it will be done for them by my Father in heaven. For where two or three gather in my name, there am I with them."

~Matthew 18 (NIV)

~~~

I spent three days alone, fasting, listening to the forgiveness series, studying God's Word, and on my knees until I came to grips with what I would need to do. Dr. Stanley would take me through a process of forgiveness. Naturally, he talked about how the blood of Christ was shed for the forgiveness of all sins – even the ones yet to be committed. He went on to explain the importance of forgiving one's self. And then, he stressed the significance of forgiving the perpetrator, even if that person was one and the same person – i.e., me.

The one exercise that Dr. Stanley suggested I felt to be especially beneficial to aid in forgiving transgressors was to take an empty chair and "invite" your perpetrator(s) to sit there. Of course, it would appear to be empty, but you would talk to your demon, or "haint," and forgive him/her for whatever wrongdoing he or she had committed against you.

~~~

Not everyone has the luxury of facing his/her demons. People sometimes die before reconciliation can occur. Some people may never feel comfortable enough, nor bold enough, to confront their assailants. The chair is an ingenious mechanism for completing the walk of full forgiveness. Dr. Stanley's series is an incredible message, and one I would recommend highly to aid in your struggle with forgiveness issues.

~~~

Now, I'll be honest: I felt foolish ... at first. *You've got to have humor in the mix here or else the message gets really heavy, so indulge me. I can't reflect on the exercise without thinking of good ol' Texas boy George Strait's "The Chair." You know the one – "Excuse me, but I think you've got my chair." Yeah, that one. But, hey, I was there searching and open to suggestions!* Nevertheless, I set "the chair" in the middle of that motel room and followed Dr. Stanley's advice. As I began to pour out my heart to this "empty demonic chair," I felt the chains loosening from around the chambers of my heart. It was cleansing, it was healing, and it was transforming for me. Nope! I didn't go through all the sordid details. It wasn't necessary. I simply forgave them with the strength of Christ. It was a telling moment. I had come clean with the goods, and the weight of years of heaviness in my heart began melting away. What an incredible feeling.

You Want Me to Do What?

But, alas ... *here we go again* ... God was not finished. There was one more leg of my journey ... one more key I would have to insert into a locked door. What – or should I say *who* – waited on the other side of that door would present me with my greatest test of faith yet to come. God had not let me down. I was all too familiar with this urging in my soul. He means what He says and says what He means. His promises were mine. I prayed for those promises, and He intended to deliver. Would I be willing to take that next step in getting past the past? My present fugitive status was about to come clean at last.

> *Not everything that goes wrong in your life is someone else's fault.*

25

Part 2: Fugitive in the Present

Clearing the Haints

It's one thing to talk to a chair; it's quite another to meet your demons eyeball to eyeball. What God had in store next for this gal was going to have to settle on the heart for a while. I'm a bold person, but it could take a month to even do what God was expecting of me. My family was scattered from here to yonder and back again. Mother had divorced Dad. She and my sister had moved, and I didn't even know where they were living. *Of course, if you closed your eyes going through Lakeland, you'd miss it. Even the rural routes are within close proximity of nowhere, so it wouldn't be an impossible task to set about. Talk about dancing around an issue with God. I was doing it.* With my brothers working, all of them married, it would take some doing to visit each one of them individually. And, Dad, well. … I gulped at the very thought.

I prayed and read the black and red ink off the pages of Matthew 5. I had not shared with Webby what I was contemplating. Not yet anyway. I needed to be resolved in my spirit that I could march in there armored up with God and not disappoint my Commander in Chief. It was important to my walk with Him. He would test my fortitude.

After wrestling down every excuse known to man not to accept the mission, God finally strong-armed me into submitting to His will. The task had been assigned to me to clear the haints, and I would set about the mission. They had set up residence in my life long enough. I loved my family. I didn't want to be estranged from any of them. God knew that. It would be one of the most difficult things I had ever faced thus far, but again, His hand of assurance rested on my shoulder. Face them, I would. Conquer my fear, He willed that. I would leave on Saturday.

~~~

Here's an exercise for you to do on your own in order to clear your haints. Take some white paper plates — cheap, white paper plates. Write across one side of your plate one or all of these: a name, date, or some word to associate a memory that has kept you a prisoner to your past. Use as many plates as you have haints. Remember, you want to clear them all out of your life.

Take your plates and scatter them writing side down about your home in a high-traffic area — in the garage, the kitchen, your living area, even on your driveway or in your yard if you feel comfortable doing so. (Make certain you place them in a place so as not to incur harm to running children or others. Alert your family they are there. You don't have to explain to anyone why they're there, unless you choose to do so. It might be healing to do that, but use your best judgment.) Wherever you decide to place them, make sure they get really grimy and soiled. Go ahead and take your foot and twist it around on top of the plates to make sure they really get good and dirty. If you have kids around, they'd love to stomp around on those plates for you a while, so let them have at it.

After these plates have been trampled on for a sufficient period of time, gather them. Take them to the dining table where you will enjoy your meal. Take them to bed with you and sleep with them under your pillow. Bring them with you in your car when you run errands. Don't forget to stuff them in your purse and let them shadow you at work. Oh, sure, go ahead: take them to the restroom and the shower. No point in leaving them behind anywhere you go. After all, they should follow you around for a while.

Next, take your plates and go through them one by one. What? You don't want to touch them? They're disgusting? Really? Of course they are. They're haints. Why do you think we're trying to get rid of the things!

Go ahead; look at the name, the date, the word that was placed on each plate. I want you to feel how comfortable it feels with your past looking back at you rather than you looking back at your past. You see, until you look it in the eyes, face it head on — not to relive the moments or the horrors of the pain it may have brought you, but just to stare it down so that you fear it no longer — you'll never walk in the present as a free person in Jesus Christ, much less the future. You cannot be as effective for Christ when you're weighted down with unforgiveness, anger, resentment, rejection, disappointment, bereavement, failure, or regret — to mention only a few. Satan knows what he's doing. He loves keeping you suppressed, feeling too unworthy to serve our Lord.

Now, say a prayer over your haints. Forgive them. Give them all to God. If there was a person(s) involved — even you — (and typically, people, not things, cause hurts), pray a blessing for his/her life.

Here comes the hardest part. These guys have been hanging around with you for a long time. You may even feel like they're part of your family, you're sidekicks. But, it's time to part ways, my friend. Put them in an appropriate fireproof container or fireplace and strike a match. Burn your plates. Clear the haints. Scatter the ashes, flush the ashes, toss the ashes. Just clear your haints. Shake the dust from your feet, and be done with the part of your past that keeps you a fugitive in your present. Get ready to be a more effective, productive person for you, your family, the Lord. They're ready for you.

~~~

… "Blessed are the poor in spirit, for theirs is the kingdom of heaven. Blessed are those who mourn, for they will be comforted. Blessed are the meek, for they will inherit the earth. Blessed are those who hunger and thirst for righteousness, for they will be filled. Blessed are the merciful, for they will be shown mercy. Blessed are the pure in heart, for they will see God. Blessed are the peacemakers, for they will be called children of God. Blessed are those who are persecuted because of righteousness, for theirs is the kingdom of heaven. ... "You have heard that it was said, 'Love your neighbor and hate your enemy.' But I tell you, love your enemies and pray for those who persecute you, that you may be children of your Father in heaven. He causes his sun to rise on the evil and the good, and sends rain on the righteous and the unrighteous.

~Matthew 5 (NIV)

26

Part 2: Fugitive in the Present

Miraculous Holy Hoedown

Shortly after God won the debate in my heart, I asked Webby for another weekend. It was time to get down South and look up the family members one by one and have my little holy hoedown with them. Webby was more than gracious, and inquired as to when "we" would leave. This one I had to do alone. He understood and was quick to remind me that God would be with me, and I wouldn't be alone.

It was a beautiful Saturday when I climbed into the Toyota Corolla to head South. Webby and I had prayed all week. No one knew but the two of us. I didn't call the family to say, "I'm coming in." I decided I would just show up. *(Learned that showing-up trick from God.)* It would take all day Saturday and probably most of Sunday to corral them all, but I was specific in how I wanted to handle it. You'll remember I believe in praying for specifics! All I can do is what I can pray *(Another story, another topic, my next book!)*, so I would get specific with God and leave the rest to Him.

I asked Webby to pray for my specifics. He smiled, kissed my forehead, and told me he would pray. I wanted each one of them in the same place without their spouses and kids. It was a tall order, I'll assure you of that! But we *are* talking about a God who can part the Red Sea, you know! We're talking about a God who loves a challenge. So, I drove out of Atlanta fully believing it would come to pass, that God would do whatever it took to accomplish the task. I didn't know how, that was His call; I just believed however it all panned out would be part of His perfect plan.

It was a beautiful day. Not a cloud in the sky from Atlanta down to Valdosta, which is not far from the Florida line. The forecast called for a gorgeous but hot late-spring day. The windows were down, the radio off – yes, off – and I was praying as I drove down Southbound 75. The four-hour trip would be filled with conversations between the Lord and me. I wouldn't rehearse the words to be spoken upon arrival; He would just provide those. I was confident in my efforts. The venture had been bathed in scalding hot prayer. I was acting on free will – the same free will that had me claim my Gideons' Bible in school. It was the same free will that I tapped to study the scriptures by flashlight while hanging onto the hope the words offered me. I had acted upon my free will to pray my way out of a seemingly hopeless situation. I was no stranger to stepping out in faith with my will intact.

Told You He'd Show Up!

Now, a Route 1 address encompasses a lot of territory. But, again, Lakeland is small. It was my time that was more limited than the territory. It didn't take me long at all to make my way to mother's hot, small, un-air-conditioned singlewide mobile home out on the rural roadway. I pulled in. She and my sister Kathy were quite surprised but thrilled to see me.

To make a long story short, one by one, my brothers began to drive by mother's mobile home that day, spotted my Atlanta tag, and dropped in to see their sister. Before the hour was up, all eight siblings were in the mobile home – devoid of spouses and children. The last to show was … yep … Junior. You got it, my dad! Had no business there, but he'd made it his business to drop in unexpectedly many times before, from what I'd heard.

It was a pretty cramped mobile home with all ten of us in the living area. Everyone was laughing and cutting up, jabbing and jawing at each other, loud, boisterous, but enjoying one another's company. By now, I was really churning inside, all the while praying, "God, give me the words and give me the strength."

Suddenly, we hear a clap of thunder that rocked the world! And then, the bottom fell out. When the bottom falls out in a mobile home, you can hardly hear yourself think. Most everyone got up saying they had to get going. I was shrieking, thinking, *No, God, they can't leave! I haven't had a chance to tell them yet. Stop them!* Someone opened the door and quickly closed it back. You could not see your hand in front of your face! Talk about the miracle storm!

He showed up! Our God of impossibles had given me a captive audience at the time I needed it. The rain would subside sometime during that hour, but no one cared. My family sat and listened intently as I shared the message of the forgiveness of Jesus Christ. I had been somewhat instrumental in the baptism of each of them, as I reminded them, because of the stripes I wore beside the road each Sunday. It was that persistence of attending church that would eventually get all of my family baptized in the Alapaha River. *(My husband had baptized my sister sometime after that.)* They would backslide on their promise to Jesus to remain faithful; thus, the reason we were going through the exercise on forgiveness again that day.

I went around to each of them and first asked for forgiveness where I had failed them, and then told each of them that I forgave them for their acts of commission and omission against me. *(At least the ones where the shoe fit.)*

But here I was, again, reintroducing them to the same saving blood of the spotless slain Lamb. This time I was sharing my testimony, my personal witness of His saving power, my account of how He had freed me from a prison of hopelessness, and how His redemption had restored me and made me a whole, functioning servant for Him. I poured out my heart to the receptive ears and hearts that day.

It would be a turning point for some, seeds planted for others. Two of them would seek rehabilitation from drugs and alcohol. My sister was a godsend. She was closely connected with these two brothers, both by distance and relationship, and would play an integral part in the healing process during their recovery. Years down the road, each of my siblings came to understand the saving grace of Christ Jesus – some of them more than others. Some, including my dad, will never be released from their silent prisons, because they have failed to forgive pain inflicted on and by them.

My four-hour drive back to Atlanta found me praising God. I was pretty pumped over His answer to the specifics, from gathering the family to the "miracle storm." It was some kind of Holy Hoedown God had orchestrated. Oddly enough, though not a bit surprising, there was no sign of rain beyond a mile of where we were. Sunny, hot, and not a drop had fallen anywhere else!

The most beautiful part was, it had stopped raining in my heart! There was no longer a heavy cloud hanging over it, smoldering me, smothering me, and canvassing my countenance. *Pop-pop, fizz-fizz, oh, what a relief it is!*

Free to Move About in the Present

When you hear the words "forgiveness is for you," it truly is. Only then are you able to move on – to unbuckle that seatbelt and move about the plane with ease. I'm rarely on an airplane and hear that message come across from the pilot that I don't relate to the freedom I experienced that day. You're free to move about in the present.

That was a real step into the present for me that day. I had completely turned in the "striped suit" I had kept under my white robe. Satan would no longer claim a stronghold in that area of my life. I could love my parents and brothers again. *My sister, being the baby, had never given me any reason to forgive her. She endured a lot like me.* I've managed to have a relationship with each of them, although it is strained with my dad. He is in his own private prison and may never step into the fullness of Light. I continue to pray for him. *He is one of God's children, too.*

I had freed myself from the past years before, but until that day, I had been a fugitive in the present. I had been an escapee, a prisoner on the run on any given day. I didn't want to be "in hiding." I wanted to *belong* to today. I wanted to be effective for Christ. Use my talents. Make a difference in someone else's life. God was calling me to greater cause. He needed me for battle. I had to keep my eyes on the goal – that target of the cross in front of me. I would no longer look back. I didn't have to see what was over my shoulder. It was no longer a threat to me.

~~~

Remember Lot's wife in Genesis 19? Of course you do. We all know that sad story. My husband and I had the opportunity to visit the Dead Sea, actually floating in it and getting a sulfur bath and mudpack; it was awesome. But to stand at the Dead Sea and the land surrounding what was Sodom and Gomorrah was amazing! It's Salt Lake City a thousand times over. It is truly beautiful barrenness. You can look out amongst the vastness of that area and see scads of pillars of salt that have accumulated from the evaporation of the water.

As I stood in awe assessing the terrain, these pillars represented vertical symbols of disobedience by Lot's wife. They were reminders of what we can become when we try to hold on to things that God purges from our lives. We keep looking back when He warns us of the inherent dangers of doing so. We may not turn into a pillar of salt, but we become immobile in His Kingdom. He calls us to be salt of the Earth – not a briny reflection of our past.

~~~

Facing my haints was difficult, but how liberating it became. I was no longer a part of the Chain Gang. I didn't have to wear the cloak of Christ over a prison uniform and run the risk of exposing a failure, weakness, or ghost from my past. I was no longer in that place – constantly looking over my shoulder to see if my past was catching up to me, nor even looking back to see what was left behind.

No longer would the memories take me by surprise.

No longer would the hurts take my heart captive and leave my emotions amuck.

No longer would the torment sneak in at night and arrest my peaceful slumber.

I was getting past the past. I was done. It was finished. Through the grace, mercy and strength of Jesus Christ, I would overcome. I was free to move about in the present.

My miracle storm was a loud, clear message from God. It was as though He was saying to me, "I'm still answering your prayer. It didn't bounce off the ceiling. It made it to my ear. I've only just begun with you, My Child. I will continue to answer that prayer until you come home."

From that day forward I began walking in the indisputable knowledge that God was sustaining me. I no longer lived as a fugitive in the present. I began realizing the fullness of His blessings.

~~~

> The LORD is my shepherd, I lack nothing.
> He makes me lie down in green pastures,
> He leads me beside quiet waters,
> He refreshes my soul.
> He guides me along the right paths
> For his name's sake.
> Even though I walk

Through the darkest valley,
I will fear no evil,
For you are with me;
Your rod and your staff,
They comfort me.

You prepare a table before me
In the presence of my enemies.
You anoint my head with oil;
My cup overflows.
Surely your goodness and love will follow me
All the days of my life,
And I will dwell in the house of the LORD forever.
~Psalm 23 (NIV)

Part 2: The Present

Life Lesson Plan 2

It is my earnest prayer that you have begun to incorporate the Evaluate Life Lesson Plan into your daily routine. You are, no doubt, beginning to experience the chains loosening that have kept your heart captive to fear, bitterness, resentment, hurt, and other emotional disturbances.

Now, we must put our hand to the plow, focus on our target – the Cross – and never look back. While you relish in the warmth of Light on your face, you modestly keep on your undergarments of the past for fear of the transparency losing them will bring. Don't be afraid to allow your spouse, a friend, or someone who loves you unconditionally to be your partner in your fugitive state. They will be supportive of helping you exchange your key of hope for your key of faith. Don't be timid about going forward. It is a leap of faith, but you have nothing to lose but your past once and for all, and a promising future to gain!

Here are your take-away tools for shedding the prison garb once and for all. Let's press onward toward the goal. Putting one haint to rest will empower you to take on others. Your confidence will emerge as you find your backbone. Your strength will come from the Word. Don't deny yourself exposure to the richness and fullness of His message daily. You are why He sent it.

Eliminate

(Read Philippians 3 – Pressing on toward the goal!)

- **Lose your fear.** Nothing can be accomplished in your life if you are stalemated by apprehension. You are not alone in your battle. God will give you the strength and the words to address issues and move on. All you have to provide is the will to do so.

- **Pray for your miraculous holy hoedown.** You can tap into God's power through the faith of a mustard seed. I find that incredibly bewildering. Imagine how many blessings we miss because we don't ask! Remember what I told you: All I can do is what I can pray!

- **Do the chair exercise.** Forgive your perpetrator(s). Hold no malice toward the offender(s). It is God's place to deal with injustices. Leave it in His capable hands. He's got the full scoop and can dispense punishment and/or mercy better than you. You have better things to concern yourself with. Move on.

- **Reevaluate your feelings.** I believe you'll sense a difference. Grade yourself. Develop a scale of freedom. Graph it and measure your progress. Forgiveness is healing, but deep wounds don't mend overnight. Ask God to be patient with you, you be patient with yourself, and then be patient on God.

- **Begin to uncover the "selfs" you lost along the way.** Reacquaint yourself with self-worth, self-confidence, self-control, self-motivation, and self-determination. Try them on for size. They'll soon take on a comfortable fit in your life, and you will be stepping to a new beat, and it won't be the sounds of "the men working on the chain-gang"!

- **Praise and pray to the One who stood in the gap for you.** He's not only your focus; He's got your back! Everything will be all right.

- **Reward yourself for progress.** Put on your best face, fancy duds, take your spouse, your friends, and/or children and celebrate! No need to tell them why unless you desire to. The change in your countenance will be evident. They'll be delighted to commemorate your occasion whether they understand the change or not. Let the world begin to see the change in you. Your witness will make the difference in someone else's life.

Part 3

Pardoned for the Future

27

Part 3: Pardoned for the Future

Dressed for the Occasion

One would have never suspected Cornelius Dupree, Jr. to be a criminal. He didn't look the type. There was no sheepish, smug aura about his endearing smile. No cause to question his sincerity. The man could have easily passed as an attorney, a politician, or a CEO of a Fortune 500 company. Fit and trim, he donned a black pin-stripe, tailored suit with tie, standing tall and blameless before the Court, attorneys, and spectators. After serving 30 years for the crimes of rape and robbery, DNA testing proved this man was innocent. He had received 75 years for a crime for which he had always maintained his innocence. Though offered the opportunity on several occasions, he adamantly refused to cut his sentence short by admitting to be a sex offender. He would suffer the consequences for someone else's injustices. One would have expected Cornelius to be bitter and angry for the egregious error that befell his fate. Rather, his attitude and demeanor that day displayed a positive outlook for his future.

On January 4, 2011, Cornelius Dupree would walk out of prison a free man. Not a parolee. Not someone who would have to look back at wasted years in a prison being punished for something he never deserved. Not exposing any leftover prison garb. Mr. Dupree was a pardoned man. He was exonerated from all association with the crime in any manner. Cornelius would emerge out of a shackled past not only into a present of hope, but fully pardoned for the future. And, Cornelius Dupree, Jr. was dressed for the occasion.

~~~

When I drove away from my experience of the miracle storm, I de-garbed. God granted me full pardon that sunny, glorious day. It would be another defining moment, another turning point, but still in battle for His cause. I found everything and anything for which to praise God on my way home. The trees, the grass, the flowers, the sky, the clouds, the air – you name it, I praised Him! I was certainly in the midst of a mountain-top experience. Thought I'd be there forever. There was nothing else that fretted me more, and so, life was going to be carefree from that moment on.

It did work out exactly as I had planned. *For a day or two, at least.* Webby was pleased to see my burdens fall away regarding my family. There would continue to be trouble with the hometown folks. I would continue to get calls from Mom about Dad's drunken binges. Although they were divorced, he still felt he retained control over everything she did.

~~~

Mother would eventually move to Atlanta and live with us until she could make it on her own. Life would always be difficult for her until she passed away. She truly never knew a minute's peace after her marriage to my father.

Her most enjoyable times were when she had her children, grands and great-grands around her. She lived to love them, and her heart was more available to take pleasure in doing so after their divorce.

~~~

Oh, yeah, surely you didn't think everybody lived happily ever after, did you? It didn't happen that way at all. Life continued as always. I shared the Word, asked for forgiveness, and had forgiven. I was free of the haints. But, the quicker you grow up, the sooner you learn that every day has its own share of haints. Therefore, my focus had to remain on one thing – seeking God every day.

~~~

> But seek first his kingdom and his righteousness,
>
> And all these things will be given to you as well.
>
> Therefore do not worry about tomorrow,
>
> For tomorrow will worry about itself.
>
> Each day has enough trouble of its own.
>
> ~Matthew 6:33-34 (NIV)

~~~

Being acquitted from the burden of my past would free up my life for greater service to God. It lightened my heart to enjoy the precious children God had entrusted to Webby and me to train up for Him. It allowed me to become a more productive and creative minister's wife. It also permitted me to begin a career that would serve not only to provide for our family but produce income for many others, as well.

Now that those dastardly undergarments of my past were no longer exposed, my life began to unfold in incredible ways. I was introduced into the world of court reporting, and very soon thereafter became a budding entrepreneur. The benefits my new career afforded me would not bear full witness for many years. Whereas its financial benefits were gratifying for an underpaid minister's lifestyle, it would be exposure to hundreds of woes of people caught up in some sordid past. These experiences would stir a melting pot of passion in me that God would ultimately use for His purpose.

I have more than adequately pulled off my "building" of a home. I have remained a bride on display long since the wedding gown was put to rest. Webby and I found the secret to being "Simply Married" *(a book the two of us are currently co-authoring)*. We ran with life and invited challenge. We have been strong leaders and willing followers. Rolling up our sleeves and cleaning toilets alongside church volunteers has kept us humble servants for our Lord. Hours of service have been poured out of our lives into service for the King. To say either of us realized how much would be demanded of us day in and day out would be less than honest. The sacrifices a minister's family makes would shatter most ordinary marriages. Those types of sacrifices continue to destroy the families of many faithful clergy warriors.

I have served God well in my role as a minister's wife. I wore the garment in fine style. Not your "typical" minister's wife look. *What is that anyway? I've been challenged by that during our entire ministry. What is a "typical" minister's wife's look? God made each of us unique. Conforming people to some mold is like stuffing their round personality into a square body. We stigmatize people when we predispose them to a certain standard. We rob them of their individuality, and stifle the positive influence they could bring in someone's life.*

I was career-oriented, and I dressed for success. Not only in the clothes I wore, but how I gave attention to detail. I was criticized for delegating jobs that needed to be accomplished, and also for how I pulled solo duty when I lacked the time to organize a team. But, I executed the responsibilities of a minister's wife in harmony with my husband's calling. It is an honor to have been selected – yes, handpicked – to team up with a minister and work side by side with him as an integral part of God's workforce. Yes, I dressed for the occasion with pride.

Likewise, my motherhood attire would fit quite nicely. Outside of grandmotherhood, there is nothing that compares to the feeling of the joys of this awesome assignment from God. Memories became my specialty. Our home was well-seasoned with laughter. Life skills were incorporated into their growing experiences. Discipline was dispensed as necessary. *Like everyone else, we had our share of seasons of growing pains with children. No, a minister's family is not immune to these kinds of trials. They're going to disappoint somewhere along the way. It's a given.* There were plenty of nourishing moments for a family living under the shelter of God's love.

There has never been a day the children in my care would have to wonder if they were loved by me. The feelings of rejection, unworthiness, and disregard by a parent never plagued one of their days. That resolve was determined years before I held them in my arms; it was pre-set in my heart as a child. *Unless one has been through an episode of abuse and/or neglect as a child, it is hard to imagine the depths of hopelessness he/she feels. Except for eternal separation from God, there is no darkness that surpasses it.*

Trust had come full circle. My trust in God had allowed my life to take an incredible journey. Stepping out of my past was only the beginning of a phenomenal future – a future that God had planned for me from the beginning. Hanging up the prison garb had allowed me to adorn myself with all the virtues of a more godly woman. Not a perfect woman, but a woman after God's own heart. I would never claim to match the qualifications of the Proverbs "virtuous woman," but my household would be one that would serve the Lord. Whatever task He assigned me, I was confident He would dress me for the occasion.

~~~

> The wise woman builds her house, but with her own hands
>
> the foolish one tears hers down.
>
> ~ Proverbs 14:1 (NIV)

> *To keep one eye on bygone days is to lose clear vision for things ahead.*

28

Part 3: Pardoned for the Future

Documented Evidence

We understand the meaning of pardon. I mean, of course, aside from the "What? Excuse me? What'd you say?" The kind of pardon of which I speak means "the act of excusing a mistake or offense," resembling when President Ford pardoned President Nixon. Pardon is also "the legal document granting release from punishment of an offense." Many times, when a President exits the Oval Office, he will grant a pardon to someone serving time in prison for some crime he/she has committed. Governors have this power, as well. But, the meaning of pardon that catches my attention is "the formal act of liberating someone."

I didn't have a formal document announcing to me or to the world that I had been set free from my past. There was no certificate. No medal of valor. It wasn't published in the papers. I wasn't interviewed by anyone about the incident. In fact, outside of Webby, it bore no significance to anyone other than me. Without some documented evidence, some factual acclamation of this extraordinary event, what proof would I have to show my exoneration of the guilt and shame of my past? I could have verbally shared with my inner circle about my pardoned experience, but after much consideration I decided to put that on hold.

~~~

I purposefully made the decision not to share details about my experiences as a child until my children were older. The intimacy I shared with God was deep. He knew my heart was not quite prepared for this kind of disclosure. He was equipping me for a time, and my time had not yet come. Seasonal distractions would detain my advent of fulfilling the purpose He had defined for me. I was confident when God felt I was ready to assist others in a healing process, He would kick in doors for me. I waited on God's timing. Had I not, my attempts would have been but failures. I was thankful for His wisdom and guidance in this area for me. In the same manner He led my soulmate to my doorstep, He would lead me to other opportunities for service.

~~~

All I had was God's written promises of redemption, or liberation. But, God's pardon for my life was real. The only evidence I would have to proclaim my freedom was to live it out in my life. I would be the walking documented evidence of God's pardon. People would only know I wore the label of "Redeemed" by the way I loved. Without that, there was no proof.

Oops, there I was again – back to my original love prayer. "Please, Lord, send me someone to teach me how to love." I was living proof that pardon had been granted to this lil' gal! God had sent all the proof I needed: I had come to know Jesus; God had sent me Webby; I had two beautiful children; I was part of the body of Christ where I fellowshipped with Christians; I got to serve God in a full-time capacity.

And, oh *my*, there I was – back to my mantel prayer! "Lord, if you will just protect me, just get me out of this prison, I will serve you for the rest of my life."

I *had* been set free! It was God's hand on my shoulder that day. His spirit was comforting my wretched soul. He staked-out a dwelling place in my heart and became my personal rearguard. Not only would He scout out my future, but He would have my back. He would guard my past from devouring me. I allowed my heart to become clay in His protective hands. Not always fitting the mold, but pliable enough to be reshaped into something of value and worthy to be called His.

I *had* been taught to love! I was a lover and wife; a doting mother who made her share of mistakes but loved my children sacrificially; a caring and involved minister's wife; a successful entrepreneur who gave away more than she'll ever make again in her life; a devoted friend to all who allowed; gave 150 percent at everything she did, and spattered it with loving kindness; a person after God's own heart and one who never ceases to praise the King. My allegiance was to Him. I was someone who was free to love because Jesus came to teach me how. And I let Him!

God had not only heard my prayers, but He had executed its perfection in a marvelous story. No, no, not a storybook one that you'll hear told on some national revue. *If you're lucky, you'll hear me speak about it sometime, though. I'm much more vivacious in person!* I am just one of millions of love stories God has orchestrated in His divine plan for mankind. Each of us has our own testimony about God's amazing acts of love and redeeming grace.

I was beginning to understand how God had definitively documented my life's path for me. I didn't need the certificate. I had all the evidence. Others would see its proof in the way I lived and loved. I was exposing Christ's garments instead of my prison garb. Hallelujah!

~~~

My faith has found a resting place,
Not in device or creed;
I trust the ever living One,
His wounds for me shall plead.

I need no other argument,
I need no other plea,
It is enough that Jesus died,
And that He died for me.

Enough for me that Jesus saves,
This ends my fear and doubt;
A sinful soul I come to Him,
He'll never cast me out.

I need no other argument,
I need no other plea,
It is enough that Jesus died,
And that He died for me.

~Lyrics by: Eliza E. Hewitt

~~~

For the grace of God has appeared that offers salvation to all people. It teaches us to say "No" to ungodliness and worldly passions, and to live self-controlled, upright and godly lives in this present age, while we wait for the blessed hope—the appearing of the glory of our great God and Savior, Jesus Christ, who gave himself for us to redeem us from all wickedness and to purify for himself a people that are his very own, eager to do what is good.

~Titus 2:11-14

29

Part 3: Pardoned for the Future

Overcomer and Overrider

No amount of wrong is too wrong to forgive. Chew on that awhile. It can be a hard hunk of gristle to choke down, depending on the wrong that's been done to or through you. We fool ourselves into thinking we don't have to forgive in order to claim the key of peace. There is no other way the key will unlock the door of peace unless you are willing to forgive – yourself and others. It's useless to keep trying to jiggle the lock; it's a total misfit.

You *will* overcome your past. But, it's much more rewarding to override it. If you're hanging onto a memory of a past, whether one from yesterday or decades ago, you have already overcome it. You *are* a survivor, just not an overrider.

I prefer to think of myself as an overrider. Not because God has favored me in any special way other than He has anyone else. I am an overrider through the strength I *allowed* myself to witness through Him. His years of preparation for my purpose were not deemed as such by me. I never saw it as "training." I thought I was just living. Once the puzzle pieces began to take on a real picture for still another plan for my life, I stepped in with great confidence that the Navigator of my existence knew what He was doing when He chose me for this new detail.

It was not enough for God that I simply overcome my past; He desired me to override it. It was clear He needed me to share with others the healing I had personally experienced. The day I felt the calling in my life to step out on faith and begin a new ministry, doubt and circumspect crept in … initially. It was time to revisit familiar scriptures for encouragement and validation.

I knew He was the God of impossibles. If He wanted me stepping out on His behalf in a more vocal manner than ever before, He would make it happen. I did question His thinking, however. "Are you sure you want me to do this, Lord? Do I have the voice for this sort of thing? I've always wanted to sing, but you've said no to that. Why this? Can I say it how You want it said? I don't speak or write as eloquently as others, and You know that well." *Don't you know that God must get tired of us whining!*

He quickly took me to Exodus 4 where Moses was at Horeb, the mountain of God (Sinai), having his own "holy hoedown" with the Lord. I guess you could say like Father, like Son – they both had a way of profoundly putting us mortals in our rightful place. *I quickly adopted this as my banner verse for my ministry – the "go" part.*

~~~

Moses said to the Lord, "O Lord, I have never been eloquent, neither in the past nor since you have spoken to your servant. I am slow of speech and tongue.

The Lord said to him, "Who gave man his mouth? Who makes him deaf or mute? Who gives him sight or makes him blind? Is it not I, the Lord? Now go; I will help you speak and will teach you what to say."

~ ~ ~

He did that for Moses. Would He do that for me? Could I be His "Mosette"? This is the same God who parted the Red Sea. The one who dropped the walls of Jericho with trumpets and a shout. This God closed the lion's mouth for Daniel; kept the fiery furnace from so much as singeing a hair on the heads of Shadrach, Meshach and Abednego. This God – my God of impossibles – sent His Son as a baby, and then He healed the lame, made the blind see, raised the dead. Would He? Could He? *With any more doubting, the better question is: Should He? So, I'll hush up now, thank you.* Of course, I would follow this God. Wouldn't you?

Writing what some considered to be controversial books on marriage was the first task on this new assignment from God. His purpose continues to be revealed in the testimonies of saved marriages and changed lives. God blended my childhood, career, and minister's wife role to introduce me to this new mission. Wife, mom and grandmom were added benefits toward my credibility. Sliding into the role of "relationship expert" on a secular television network was no surprise to Him; the rest of us were pleasantly astounded. Writing a monthly *Just Ask Joyce*™ column for *Today's Woman* magazine became another opportunity to share godly principles for preservation of family history. Currently, as a Christian talk-show host for the *Just Ask Joyce Show*, I am promoting strong family values and offering advice and encouragement to hurting people. I am learning to expect the unexpected when God decides you have climbed on board with His plan for your life. He moves mountains, kicks in dead-bolted doors, and introduces you to other warriors fighting for His common cause. When He wants a job done, stand back and let Him make it happen through you. He doesn't mess around.

Singled Out

Realizing God's ways are much different from man's gives you a different mindset as to why God would single-out individuals to carry out His work here on Earth. The worldly wisdom tells us the extraordinary people are called to perform such tasks. It will also try to convince you that it takes a significant amount of resources to be successful. That's exactly what the world would want you to think. Conversely, God often chooses ordinary people to fulfill His purposes. You are as likely a candidate as this abused tobacco farm gal who was thrown into the arms of a youth minister with a stitched-up heart, fashioned into a mom/grandmom, groomed into entrepreneurship, plunged into a ministry promoting family preservation, and sculpted to write about how to "keep his pants on"! *I mean, think about that hodgepodge of unlikely characters all rolled into one. God does have a sense of humor.*

Peter and John were singled out to come before the Sanhedrin. They had been put in jail until they were questioned the next day regarding the Apostles' teaching about the resurrected Christ. These common, ordinary men had been chosen by Christ for such a time as they would have to defend His truth. This was one of those hallmark occasions. Christ knew these men would be bold. *He also knew Peter would be cowardly before he found his steadfast courage.* They didn't waver in their conviction, because they had lived the truth. They had the evidence of His liberating freedom. They were planted and would not be moved. It doesn't take extraordinary; it simply demands a strong belief system.

~~~

... "Salvation is found in no one else, for there is no other name under heaven given to men by which we must be saved." When they saw the courage of Peter and John and realized that they were unschooled, ordinary men, they were astonished and they took note that these men had been with Jesus.   ~Acts 4:12-13 (NIV)

~~~

He Gets the Job Done

God also singles out people who don't have an abundance of resources available to them in order to achieve His purposes. *I am definitely one of those!* Life experiences are often the best teacher and sometimes lend more credibility. It doesn't necessarily require one to have plentiful financial reserves to take on huge undertakings for the Lord. If He wants a mission accomplished to which He has earmarked for you, He will provide the way and means.

~~~

> For this reason I kneel before the Father, from whom every family in heaven and on earth derives its name. I pray that out of his glorious riches he may strengthen you with power through his Spirit in your inner being, so that Christ may dwell in your hearts through faith. And I pray that you, being rooted and established in love, may have power, together with all the Lord's holy people, to grasp how wide and long and high and deep is the love of Christ, and to know this love that surpasses knowledge—that you may be filled to the measure of all the fullness of God. Now to him who is able to do immeasurably more than all we ask or imagine, according to his power that is at work within us, to him be glory in the church and in Christ Jesus throughout all generations, forever and ever! Amen.
>
> ~Ephesians 3:14-21

~~~

Willing Overrider

It doesn't take outstanding qualities to serve God. But, as I mentioned earlier, you can't be effective when you're chained to the past. His desire is for you to become an overcomer, and then willingly to allow your testimony to be used to liberate others in His name. He wants your natural abilities – those talents He gifted you with, and those He didn't but will supply. He needs willing, untiring souls who will not only overcome, but will also override the penchant to look back once they've set their hand to the plow.

~~~

Bertha Smith was a missionary to China. She was near 50 years old when the Southern Baptist changed their policy that forbad women to serve on a mission field. After serving over 40 years in China, Bertha came back to the United States. When she was 93, she returned and spent her remaining days in the States praying for and ministering to pastors and other Christians. She lived to be 100, but had appointments to preach until she was 105 years old. (Can you imagine?) Bertha Smith is the personification of a willing servant for Christ. Her secret for being so active: Laboring for Jesus. It keeps you young a long time. (I want to be like Bertha!)

~~~

God is not looking for you to impress; He's looking for you to express. Express your willingness to serve Him. Express your willingness humbly to submit to His plan for your life. Express your witness to His divine power and saving grace in your life. Express your experience from being prisoner to the past, fugitive in the present, all the way to being pardoned for the future. Tell the world how He not only made you an overcomer, but how you became a *willing* overrider, because God delights in your greatness. He had a big hand in it. Now give Him one.

30

Part 3: Pardoned for the Future

Disappointing God

"Get me Charlie."

"Charlie, Lord? Are you sure?"

"Yeah, pretty sure. Is there a problem?"

"Well, Lord, Charlie hasn't earned his wings yet. Clarence took him out, and he didn't fare too well. The poor girl you assigned him to, well, she kept climbing back into the past. Charlie did the best he could, but he failed, Lord."

"No, Charlie didn't fail. Get me Charlie, Gabriel. She's got one foot out the door again."

~~~

Shedding prison garments to get outfitted for God would encompass a lot of years, and a lot of guardian angels for this farm girl! Seasons of distraction would deter God's ultimate objective for my life. Looking back, I am thankful for His patience. I'm grateful for His second chances. I'm blessed because He never gave up on me. I often wonder how many times He must have had to send a "Charlie" down to get his wings and help fix some problem with this "George Bailey." I certainly made a mess of a few things along the way. That's what seasons of distraction can do for a gal.

My best days were when I basked in God's word. The erratic nature of my business found me doling out more time to work than I had in a day. *I tease and tell people I've always managed to squeeze 37 hours out of a 24-hour day! Truth is, I did about 37 hours' worth of work in that given timeslot. Told you the farm gave me some good work ethics.* My faith was grounded, I had a heart for God, but the monster I couldn't put to rest had, by default, become my central focus.

The past no longer haunted me. Life was settling down with family. Dad found other wives he could beat up. *(Yes, unfortunately, he did on up into his old age.)* Mother struggled with health, living in low-income housing, making ends meet with the help of some of her children. Friends would come and go. I disappointed many people; they disappointed me. A drastic move away from our home state and a daughter in college would be life-altering for us all. Hardships came frequently. They still do.

Disappointing others and being disappointed was not my biggest pitfall. It was my fear of disappointing God that set me back a notch or two. I found I was getting caught up in *present pasts*. Self-defeating emotions would surface and find themselves setting blockades in my effectiveness for God. My testimony would weaken. His light in my life would go dim. I was going through the motions of being set free, yet not wearing the full garment of Christianity. I was a good person. I served. I worked my tail off in church, striving to be a support to my husband's call in the ministry. After all, I had been there with him for more than a quarter century already. *Goodness, did I just confess that? I sound ancient!*

The Walk

Underneath the surface of this good Christian, set-free, past-redeemed, abused girl from the tobacco farm were seeds of resentment for all we had sacrificed as a family. I wanted to preserve the closeness, the bond, the oneness we shared. I had envisioned my girls growing up and living nearby; having our grandchildren, and then watching those kids' ballgames and school plays and recitals, grabbing hugs and loves on a daily (at least four-times-a-week) basis. I never factored in *this* cost of serving God. It would take its toll on our children, as well. Sisters who have always been best of friends would be divided by distance; cousins who love each other dearly only infrequently enjoying one another's company. The pain was deep. It was fierce. It felt wrong.

~~~

"Walk with me, Joyce." His voice was still and low. We'd had many conversations in the past, so I knew whatever was shared would be beneficial. We began walking. "Let me tell you a story. Long ago I shared oneness with my family, too. My home was comfortable, my surroundings familiar, I had everything one could ask for. I could meet with my family anytime. Touch them. Laugh with them. Share. In obedience to God, I picked up and moved. It wasn't something I was crazy about, but I willingly obeyed. The move was a huge sacrifice, but I knew He needed me. He had singled me out to do the job; no one else could have pulled it off but me.

"I left my home, stayed gone for many years. Oh, yeah, I stayed in touch with home. I wasn't cut off from my family at all. Didn't get to visit. It was too far to travel, but we talked every day. The worst part was, not many people accepted me. I felt like a stranger in a faraway land. And then, the more I served Him, the more disgruntled people became. I couldn't win. But, I wasn't called to win. I was called to serve. I was called to love. I was called to forgive. I was called to carry a cross.

And then, when I had fulfilled God's mission, I got to go back home. So, don't fret about the cost of your service. It's all worth it in the end. Your family will be there whenever you return. I'm sitting at the right hand of my Father today."

~~~

Sometimes at your lowest moments, when you feel as though you have disappointed God to the point of uselessness, Jesus walks in the garden with you. I shared many of those private moments with this Friend. There's no level of disappointment that will bar us forever from rejoining His cause. We always have the freedom through His redemption to return to a full-serving capacity.

We hear more and more frequently how clergy are falling away from the standards of godly living. We also hear instances of where they have repented of their deeds and come back a bit more humble but a lot more impactful in their servitude. God loves the return of all degrees of prodigal children. He is also patient to wait on us to step out of that prison of the past once and for all and to decide we're giving our efforts to Him 100 percent.

God's forgiveness is far-reaching. His disappointment in our weakness as humans does not override His grace and mercy. It is our unrelenting penchant to our sinful nature that evokes His just and fair judgment.

~~~

Jesus answered them, "It is not the healthy who need a doctor, but the sick. I have not come to call the righteous, but sinners to repentance."

~Luke 5:31-32 (NIV)

~~~

A Withering Past

I texted Webby after a private moment with the Lord one morning. My message was simple:

"Need 2 go c my dad."

"What time do u want 2 leave?" *(He really meant it.)*

"Not 2day. Soon."

"lmk when ur ready. I'm n."

I didn't understand why the Holy Spirit urged me in this manner that particular day. I only knew I would obey. We would leave after Christmas. In the meantime, I would pray for God to settle my heart as to what I should say, what the purpose of this mission would be, and to cause me be tender-spirited.

I had not seen my dad since my sister-in-law passed away, only a few months after my mother had died. We had talked quite awhile at the hospital when Mother was ill. Tension was high, and so was he. It turned out to be a fruitless convergence of the two personalities.

Driving up to his home was uneventful. He was expecting us, and excited for the visit. I wasn't surprised at how the years had aged him; we all take on shades of maturity. Nor did it surprise me the toll the liquor had taken. He was still a drinker, but not hitting the bottle as fiercely these days. His warm demeanor was of no consequence either. Anytime he saw me, he embraced like we were best of friends. What did surprise me, however, was what he led us to before we barely stepped one foot over the threshold. Pictures. Pictures of family. A picture of all eight kids when we were much (*much*) younger. Pictures of every grandchild – very outdated. Even great-grands. *My clan was missing in the lot of multitudes of great-grands. My bad. I've since remedied that. They are a part of the family tree, too.*

"Do you know who that is?" and he pointed to a tiny, black-and-white, wallet-size photo.

"Uh, well, yeah," I chimed in. "That's Mother!"

"And me," he quickly added.

"Well, yeah, I see that."

"That was the day we got married." I didn't have to look for the pride; it spilled forth readily.

"Who took this picture?" I asked.

"Her Maw."

My eyes smarted. "She was so beautiful," I whispered.

"Yeah, we made a pretty pair."

And, he was right. They were a handsome-looking couple. He went on talking about other pictures. I was frozen in the moment, just studying Mother's eyes. There was such uncertainty there. Such longing. An innocence of youth . She was standing out in front of my dad; in close proximity, but not resting on him, not touching him at all. Just standing there in her aloneness.

~~~

I wonder if she knew it was despair attaching itself to her. From that moment on, she would know nothing but loneliness. She was always alone in her sorrow. Single-handedly battling her anger. A prisoner to pain. She would know not one moment's peace from that day forward. Some of the stories she shared with me, I often wonder why she did. I wish she hadn't. I knew enough of my own. Except when she shared, I knew how to pray for her. And so, I did. I prayed for God to release her from her demons, and that she would find rest from the nights they would revisit her long after she was alone ... again.

Mother would never experience a life outside her private prison. Never walked out of her past. Anytime you spoke with her, the conversation always reverted to the past. The past was her present, and it was her tomorrow, as well.

She had known the Lord. Honored Him more in her later years. The crying shame was that my mother was a willing servant with much to give. Frustration and pain snuffed out her light for the Lord for many years. She lived to love, loved to live, and died because both had taken their toll. What a waste of good warrior material.

~~~

"And, you remember who this is?" he asked, as he pointed to a group shot of an ensemble.

My blood ran cold. "Oh, yeah, I remember."

He rambled on about the names of the group, as though it was some hallmark memory that we should be proud of.

"Lord, keep me tender-spirited," I prayed silently.

It was an 8x10 black-and-white photo that hung proudly against the nicotine-stained walls. I fully expected the memory of "the kiss" to incite my better senses. Instead, I took a seat on the couch, and gently redirected the conversation.

Again, God's protection intervened. A quiet peace invaded my spirit. My blood still ran cold at the thought, but it was not at all how I expected I might react. Confirmation. Victorious confirmation. Yes! Yes! I truly was pardoned for the future. The past memory didn't weigh down my countenance. I wasn't looking over my shoulder for the next memory to pop up; we continued to talk. It was documented evidence of His supreme victory in getting me past my past.

~~~

Hallelujah, Lord! We did it. All these years You were patient with me. You waited on me, never giving up. Thank You, God, for knowing me so intimately. Thank You for caring so deeply that You would stick with someone as undeserving of Your favor. Thank You, Lord!

Oh, and ... thank you, "Charlie"!

~~~

Junior would talk incessantly to four patient ears. Webby was so kind and gentle. A knowledge-filled son-in-law with a true preacher's heart. *Well, at least, he had partial knowledge of my past.* He was gracious and tender to Dad; supportive and attentive to me. Dad shared all his ailments; he was suffering from many. His mind was still intact, but stuck in his withering past.

We spent several hours with Dad. Took him to lunch. One of my brothers was able to join us, and, as always, it was a delightful visit with him. *We've always enjoyed a wonderful relationship.* Webby and I had both agreed we wouldn't leave without probing Dad about his salvation. I had prayed God would afford us the opportunity. Sometimes you have to make those opportunities available to you. I suspicioned it would be a topic Dad would just as soon avoid. I was right.

"Are you still going to church?"

"I can't go because the lights are too bright for my eyes," and the battle was on. *He did have a severe eye deficiency, but the lights in the restaurant were never at issue.* The conversation went downhill from there. The temperature of his tenor dropped by degrees. The tone in his voice sharpened. Webby and I met great resistance at every angle of approach. It became increasingly clear that he would have no part of discussing his salvation with us. We made more small-talk, hugged, and drove away realizing it might possibly be the last visit I would ever get to share with my father.

Silence abounded. I needed to assess the situation. Webby allowed that; he knows me well. My initial thought: *Are you disappointed God? Could I have done more?* I dismissed the notion, and prayed for my dad instead.

After a while, Webby broke the silence in his usual insightful support. He reminded me of what Christ said to the Apostles when He sent them out on a mission to the "lost sheep of Israel." Jesus had given them authority to perform miracles – "to drive out impure spirits and heal every disease and sickness." Before they left, He gave them these instructions:

~~~

"As you go, proclaim this message: 'The kingdom of heaven has come near.' Heal the sick, raise the dead, cleanse those who have leprosy, drive out demons. Freely you have received; freely give. "Do not get any gold or silver or copper to take with you in your belts— no bag for the journey or extra shirt or sandals or a staff, for the worker is worth his keep. Whatever town or village you enter, search there for some worthy person and stay at their house until you leave. As you enter the home, give it your greeting. If the home is deserving, let your peace rest on it; if it is not, let your peace return to you. If anyone will not welcome you or listen to your words, leave that home or town and shake the dust off your feet. Truly I tell you, it will be more bearable for Sodom and Gomorrah on the day of judgment than for that town."

~Matthew 10-7-15 (NIV)

Pressing On

Webby reminded me that not everyone will be receptive to the message of salvation. We had experienced that many times throughout the years in our ministry together. It's difficult to convince people what they must let go of in order to receive the kind of freedom that Jesus offers. He also reminded me that we can't judge another's heart. That reminder was extremely comforting.

When you're in battle for His cause, you don't always pull in the flock. Some will not be won over by you, although you may plant a seed that will be nurtured by another later. But when someone rejects the Gospel message and is unreceptive to lend an ear, we need to move on to fertile ground. There is much to do for His Kingdom.

Webby was right – it's not our place to judge a person's heart; that is within God's authority alone. Our position is to live out the love of Christ, offer the message of salvation, and be a support to those with one foot out of the past.

God is not disappointed when we don't win a soul to Him. His disappointment comes when we never try.

~~~

> Not that I have already obtained all this, or have already arrived at my goal, but I press on to take hold of that for which Christ Jesus took hold of me. Brothers and sisters, I do not consider myself yet to have taken hold of it. But one thing I do: Forgetting what is behind and straining toward what is ahead, I press on toward the goal to win the prize for which God has called me heavenward in Christ Jesus.
> ~Philippians 3:12-14

> God means what He says and says what He means.

31

Part 3: Pardoned for the Future

Key of Peace

Imagine having the knowledge about the transformation that took place in my life, not to mention the countless lives you have read about, heard of, and even personally witnessed being transformed, yet walking away and failing to pick up the key of peace. *You thought I'd forgotten about this key, didn't you? Nope. Intentionally saved it for last.*

I would be sorely remiss should I not, once again, share the only true source for ultimate freedom. Not just from some daunting past, but for today, and every tomorrow you have. And oh, yes,

227

despite the misnomer than none of us are promised a tomorrow, you can rest assured – there will be one.

Laying claim to the Key of Peace doesn't just involve receiving Christ in your life. Many Christians are stumbling around churches dragging their ball-and-chained past with them. Yes, we must understand Jesus went to the cross for the redemption from sin, but that act also brings healing. The message of forgiveness is that it takes care of the past – it's all over. *Finis!* His redemption not only gives you grace, but it gives you the ability to give grace, as well. And, love. And, to be loved.

Often, the reason people can't get past their past is they never reach the point to give grace. Jesus was mistreated, but He gave grace. He was wronged, but He forgave. Because He did, you not only have the capacity to survive, you have the capacity to surpass – to give grace to others. When we have the capacity to forgive people that wrong us, we truly are set free in Christ. When you're free in Christ, you are free indeed.

~~~

> Jesus replied, "Very truly I tell you, everyone who sins is a slave to sin. Now, a slave has no permanent place in the family, but a son belongs to it forever. So if the Son sets you free, you will be free indeed."
>
> ~John 8:34-36 (NIV)

~~~

It should be enough for us to know that His blood was spilled to relieve us of the burden of sin – ours or someone else's inflicted upon us. We don't know why God would sacrifice something as special as His only begotten Son. It is a forfeiture we may never fully comprehend. We can't imagine why anyone would *agree* to suffer such a heinous death for the sins of everyone – those deceased, those living, and the yet-to-be born. How can anyone love us that much? It's a simple answer. He just does.

~~~

When our girls were young, I would fire questions at them about why they love certain people. I wanted them to develop the skill and freedom to express their love and appreciation for people. I've done the same with our grandchildren. It's a great ingredient in the nurturing of tenderness and communication in relationships.

Our oldest grandchild, Connor, is a very precocious child – wise beyond his years. He had just turned three when he bowled me over with his childlike wisdom. He climbed up Mimi's legs like a tree trunk, and I cradled him in my arms as he straddled my hips, locking his legs securely around my waist. His arms were wrapped tightly around my neck, hugging and generously dispensing kisses.

I have a game I play with them – my "Who do you love?" game.

"Who do you love?" I asked.

"Mimi," Connor replied. And I dipped him down and swooped him back up again.

"Who does Mimi love?"

"Connor," he replied, grinning. Another dip, swoop, and a big giggle.

"Come on, now, who do you love?"

"I love you, Mimi," he reminded me. Another reward.

Then, more seriously, "Why do you love me, Connor?"

"I don't know."

"Sure you know, Connor. Why do you love Mimi?"

"Mimi, I don't know, I just do."

"No, you have to know why you love me. You have to tell me. Why do you love Mimi?"

"Mimi, I don't know why I love you, I just do. Isn't that enough?"

Talk about profound! My knees were rubbery, my face all blubbery, but that was exactly enough for me.

~~~

Your Past Molds Today, Today Shapes Tomorrow

I'm often asked if I could change one thing about my childhood, what it would be. My knee-jerk response: Nothing. If I thought for one second that anything I went through as a child would alter my relationship, my dependency, and my trust in the Lord Jesus Christ today, I wouldn't go back and change one single thing that happened to me. Any alteration in the course of my history might possibly have never brought me the husband I have. Had that not been possible, I would not have known the joys our daughters have brought. And, that would have altered the lives of my fabulous sons-in-law; how different their lives would be. And, of course, the exquisite blend of our grandchildren has enriched all our lives. Pages and decades of history obliterated? Nah, I don't think so. *That's definitely an "It's a Wonderful Life" experience to consider!*

I believe that every experience you have and every person you meet plays a role in the shaping of your future – some more significantly than others. But, those who cross our paths, and especially those who leave indelible memories, each become part of the fingerprints of who we are. They identify our persona. Those experiences become not only what make us, but also what we make of them.

My past molded me into what I am today, but my present is shaping my future. I want to do today better than I did yesterday so that my tomorrow is even brighter than today. *Don't ask me to say that again.* That's the way pardoned people live life, even when life happens harder than you had anticipated. Don't ever look back. Keep your hand to the plow and focus on Jesus.

~~~

Keep this daily exercise in mind. When you wake up each morning, lock in on your target. Take a moment to pray, thanking God for the night and for giving you another day. Here's my routine:

"Lord, I hope this day is good" *is my first petition to Him.* "Let me embrace this day you've given me with fervor and a positive attitude. Let it be to Your glory and honor, Lord, for today is tomorrow's past **and** tomorrow's future. Help me make it a good memory in every opportunity You give me. Amen."

It's a short conversation I have with God. Just the two of us in the stillness of the morning. As I've allowed myself to expand into the maturity of being a slave only to God's service, this ritual has been a rich unfolding of God's truths for the path He has designed for me.

So, try it on for size. Give it a week, at least, and see how your todays become better pasts and brighter futures.

~~~

God desires to liberate you. He wants us to be effective Christians, not a prisoner to our past, not a fugitive in the present, but pardoned for a future that will hold lasting value for us and those we touch. No sin is too great for Him to wash away. No assault too great to heal. He is our God of impossibles who holds the Key of Peace for you. His provision for our past, present and future was planned long, long ago. Our omniscient, omnipotent, and omnipresent God would understand the need for restoration in our lives.

Don't let your past keep you from experiencing the richness and flavor of God's plan for you here on Earth, and especially your hereafter. Oh, yes, God has planned an eternity for each one of us. No one will escape that episode in life. It's all a matter of where you want to spend yours – Heaven or Hell. There'll be a ticket bound for one of those two places waiting for you at your demise or Jesus' return, whichever comes first. It's a one-way route, no change of location once we arrive, so we'd better like the climate once we get there!

~~~

"Why would you want to free me from my past, Lord?"

"Because I love you."

"Why would you want to walk with me in the present, Lord?"

"Because I love you."

"Why would you want to bless me in the future, Lord?"

"Because I love you."

"Why do you love me, Lord?"

"I just do. Isn't that enough?"

~~~

… Jesus said, "If you hold to my teaching, you are really my disciples. Then you will know the truth and the truth will set you free."

~John 8:31-32 (NIV)

Part 3: The Future

Life Lesson Plan 3

You have begun to Evaluate and Eliminate past encumbrances. These exercises work anytime a past presents itself. Practice it as routinely as necessary. Prayerfully, as you grow in knowledge and deed through living out a godly life, you will stay Elevated in your walk with Christ. The ideal relationship with Him is to continue maturing in your spiritual journey.

Reflecting His love to others is a sure sign of growth. Each of us will fall short of His commands. We are human; we will continue to be imperfect here on Earth. We press on, and as we become stronger and richer in our faith, it becomes second nature for us to exhibit the fruit of the Spirit – love, joy, peace, forbearance, kindness, goodness, and faithfulness. Life takes on a new meaning when we take on the image of Christ.

Never stop hungering for God. He desires you to know Him on an intimate level, one in which He can elevate you to greatness. He desires you to experience a level of devotion so that you will come to appreciate His smallest blessings as a great prize of your allegiance to Him. His mercies a plentiful, but He is jealous. He has set you free to walk with Him, not to serve other gods.

Put into practice these take-away tools in order to Elevate yourself in your personal growth with Christ. It's a Life Lesson Plan well worth the investment. Today is tomorrow's past. Plant pleasant seeds for which to pluck fond memories. That's a past you'll learn to cherish in your present and your future. Today is also tomorrow's future. And remember, you have been pardoned for that day!

Elevate

(Read I Peter 1 – Redeemed with the precious blood of Christ!)

- **Dress for success.** You can now wear the cloak of Christ without fear your underwear is slipping! Make meaningful decisions about how you will live your life, rear your children, love your spouse and family, and how you embrace your career and life choices. You are a new creature – exonerated, pardoned, no record of wrong. Now, live that life in your walk.

- **Wait on God's timing.** Don't rush into your future. You've just rid yourself of a daunting past, stepped out of the fugitive status, so relax and seek God's clear direction for your life. Commit your future to prayer and watch the puzzle pieces begin to fall into place as He unfolds more blessings than you ever dreamed you deserved.

- **Learn to trust again.** Trust will come full circle. You *will* give your heart again. It is likely to get broken again, but it won't get shattered. Not this time. There is a new guard standing watch at your heart's door. Oh, yeah, He's the same one who's had your back all along. Now that He's your focus, He's taken up residence. Quite a different feeling!

- **Don't live with the regret of not offering Christ.** Do your best at promoting healing, forgiveness, repentance and salvation to others. God is never disappointed in you when someone's heart is unreceptive to Him when you've presented the Gospel message; only if you don't ever try. You are not the Judge. Rejoice in that.

- **Don't try to impress God; just express God through your life.** Your liberation came at great price. Live like you believe it.

- **Claim your Key of Peace.** Yes, other adversities will come and go. Because they do, your character can grow stronger in Christ if you hold on tight to peace as you continue to grow in your daily walk and Bible study.

- **Remember: Your past molds today, today shapes tomorrow.** Embrace every day with praise to God for opportunities to serve Him. Ask for strength and purpose for the day He has granted you. Your attitude will set your altitude for the day. And many times, you can alter the attitudes of those around you.

- **Remind yourself that He loves you, and that is enough.** When you Elevate yourself in His love and keep your allegiance only to Him, there is nothing you and God can't handle together. No past – whether yesterday or twenty years ago – will ever keep you hostage again. You are a Child of the King!

~~~

God is not looking for you to impress; He's looking for you to express.

In Battle for His Cause

Logan could no longer share with the listening audience. His emotions overcame his ability to communicate his elation.

"What a great testimony, Logan! You and your wife laid the foundation for your son; you trained him up in God's way. Yes, he departed for a while. You guys never ceased praying and you kept him protected through this homosexual lifestyle he was leading, but now he's back! Praise God, and kudos to you and your wife! Your prodigal son has returned. Just goes to validate God's ancient words. I'll keep you all in my prayers. God bless you, My Friend."

~~~

Another day filled with concern and victories on The Just Ask Joyce Show. Catch-All Fridays are always a toss-up. Calls focused on the targeted subjects of same-sex marriage and the adult entertainment industry, both issues that are ravaging even Christian families. Another bold and beneficial day for Christ. Tony, Logan, Leann, Colleen, and Verlin — a lot of calls for an hour-long show, but not unusual. There's much talk about expanding it to two. God will let me know when it's time.

The past couple weeks have been filled with topics surrounding restoration and preservation of the family unit. Information equipping parents with daily struggles. Alternatives to health issues like ADHD, arthritis and prostate problems. Local guests quickly gaining national recognition – the Soetes, married forty-seven plus years. They survived infidelity involving a family friend at their twenty-year mark with six children from their union. These kinds of real-life stories offer hope to the hundreds dealing with forgiveness after betrayal. National guests like Dr. Emerson Eggerichs bringing expert advice about honoring the covenant relationship through his book Love and Respect; Dr. Glenn Stanton, Director of Family Formations for Focus on the Family spotlighting his book Secure Daughters, Confident Sons; Kay Arthur delivering a powerful message of Marriage Without Regrets; Chip Ingram elaborating on House or Home? and countless others. Nourishing families one day at a time. Enriching homes with God's Word. Question-and-answer days with me offering solutions for all sorts of matters of the heart.

There will be numerous emails waiting in my inbox – those thanking me for my boldness, as well as those pleading for help. It's the weekend, and I must begin preparing for next week's shows, and continue planning for those three months out, as well as make time for my own family – and that I make certain happens. But, my day would not be over until every email was addressed. So many of them; only one of me. My prayer has become, "Lord, expand my time, I have enough territory."

Puzzle pieces continue to fall in place – the lifetime preparation for my service to God. The mantel prayer was surely the beginning. Or, was it the Gideons? And then, my send-me-someone-to-teach-me-how-to-love prayer could have launched me to this place. Then again, perhaps it was at the hospital when I received my name. There **is** something in a name. None of it was a mistake. God has orchestrated everything. Not the injustices that befell me as a child. Those things don't come from our loving Heavenly Father. No, it was His hand that protected me. It was His protection that took the ache out of this heart and replaced it with fervor to loosen my shackles, the capacity to love, the desire to serve, and the yearning to walk in His freedom. He is my Sunrise Love, and it is true all my days are written in His book. I **am** fearfully and wonderfully made. My name … Joyce …was on His breath before it was ever on my earthly father's. God had plans for this gal. I wonder who He would have used had I not been willing?

~~~

"That's all we have time for today, Guys. Appreciate your calls. I'll be back tomorrow, same time, same great station, bringing you more take-away tools straight from my heart. I'm Joyce Oglesby, your family nourishment provider, and host of *Just Ask Joyce*™. As you know, I love my Lord, and I'm in Battle for His Cause."

For God so loved ME that He gave His only Son to teach me how to love.

Works Cited

Bible Gateway, scripture references;
http://www.biblegateway.com/passage/NIV.

Lyrics to "Onward, Christian Soldiers,"
http://library.timelesstruths.org/music/Onward_Christian_Soldiers.

Lyrics to "I Need No Other Argument,"
http://www.cyberhymnal.org/htm/m/y/myfaithh.htm.

Lyrics to, "To God Be the Glory,"
http://www.faithalone.org/journal/1996i/Ward.html.

Stanley, Dr. Charles, *A Touch of His Freedom*, JAMC, May 10, 2005, 1 72 (10), 12.

The Washington Times, "30 Years for a Crime He Didn't Commit,"
http://www.washingtontimes.com/news/2011/jan/4/dna-clears-texas-man-who-spent-30-years-prison/.

Made in the USA
Charleston, SC
25 November 2011